DK EYEWITNESS

TOP 10 TOKYO

Top 10 Tokyo Highlights

Welcome to Tokyo ... **5**
Exploring Tokyo ... **6**
Tokyo Highlights ... **10**
Imperial Palace Grounds ... **12**
Senso-ji Temple ... **14**
Sumida River ... **16**
Nihonbashi ... **18**
Ueno Park ... **20**
Tokyo National Museum ... **24**
Koishikawa Koraku-en Garden ... **28**
Meiji Jingu Shrine ... **30**
Yanaka ... **32**
Odaiba Island ... **34**

The Top 10 of Everything

Moments in History ... **38**
Historic Buildings ... **40**
Places of Worship ... **42**
Museums ... **44**
Art Galleries ... **46**
Modern and Contemporary Buildings ... **48**
Gardens and Parks ... **50**
Off the Beaten Path ... **52**
Children's Attractions ... **54**
Pop Culture Venues ... **56**
Entertainment Venues ... **58**
Onsen and Sento ... **60**
Restaurants ... **62**
Cafés and Bars ... **64**
Markets, Stores, and Shopping Streets ... **66**
Tokyo for Free ... **68**
Festivals and Events ... **70**

CONTENTS

Tokyo Area by Area

Central Tokyo 74
Ginza 80
Ueno, Asakusa, and Oshiage 86
Roppongi and Akasaka 94
Aoyama, Harajuku, and Shibuya 100
Shinjuku 106
Farther Afield 112

Streetsmart

Getting Around 120
Practical Information 124
Places to Stay 128

General Index 134
Acknowledgments 139
Phrase Book 141

Within each Top 10 list in this book, no hierarchy of quality or popularity is implied. All 10 are, in the editor's opinion, of roughly equal merit. Throughout this book, floors are referred to in accordance with American usage, i.e., the first floor is at ground level.

Title page, front cover, and spine *A vibrant street in Akihabara, a famous hub for electronics and pop culture goods*
Back cover, clockwise from top left *Cherry trees line Meguro River; Tokyo skyline with Rainbow Bridge and the iconic Tokyo Tower; Sushi rolls served with tea; a shopping street in Akihabara; Senso-ji Temple*

The rapid rate at which the world is changing is constantly keeping the DK Eyewitness team on our toes. While we've worked hard to ensure that this edition of Tokyo is accurate and up-to-date, we know that opening hours alter, standards shift, prices fluctuate, places close and new ones pop up in their stead. So, if you notice we've got something wrong or left something out, we want to hear about it. Please get in touch at **travelguides@dk.com**

ラッキー
B1
無料案内所
ゲーム
メンズサウナ
DINING BAR

Welcome to Tokyo

Everything that is both traditional and modern about Japan is found in Tokyo. It's a city of amazing architecture and fashion, delicious cuisine, and cutting-edge technology. Artistic and cultural traditions have been honed to perfection but the city is also a master of innovation and reinvention. With DK Eyewitness Top 10 Tokyo, it's yours to explore.

You may have in mind the Tokyo of popular imagination, a perpetually buzzing, utterly contemporary metropolis, illuminated by neon. But this is also a city of tranquil gardens, ancient temples, and shrines, such as the **Koishikawa Koraku-en Garden** and **Meiji Jingu Shrine**. Prepare to be beguiled by the beauty of traditional arts and crafts available to view in museums or buy in stores that have been tended by the same families for generations.

And then there is the food. The famous fish market may have moved to a new location in Toyosu but many specialist food stores remain in the Tsukiji area, an ideal introduction to Japan's unique culinary culture. The tastes of Edo – the old name for the capital – linger in the backstreets of **Yanaka** and the precincts of **Asakusa**. Best of all, despite its sprawling size and millions of inhabitants, Tokyo works like a dream. Public transportation is fast, efficient, and inexpensive. Polite service is a given, as are clean streets that are safe to walk any time of the day or night.

Whether you're visiting for a weekend or a week, our Top 10 guide brings together the best of everything the city has to offer, from the glitz of **Ginza** to the street fashion of **Shibuya**. The guide has useful tips throughout, from seeking out what's free to places off the beaten path, plus nine easy-to-follow itineraries designed to tie together a clutch of sights in a short space of time. Add inspiring photography and detailed maps, and you've got the essential pocket-sized travel companion. **Enjoy the book, and enjoy Tokyo**.

Clockwise from top: **Senso-ji Temple, exhibit at the Kite Museum, National Art Center, skyline with Mt Fuji behind, Daibutsu Buddha at Kamakura, Kabukicho district, Chidorigafuchi moat**

Exploring Tokyo

Don't be fazed by Tokyo's size and variety of attractions. The following itineraries include the very best sights in this fascinating, multi-layered city. There's also time for shopping, relaxing, and savoring Tokyo's delicious culinary scene.

Ameyoko Market has over 500 stalls and stores.

Senso-ji Temple's Hozo-mon Gate is a striking structure.

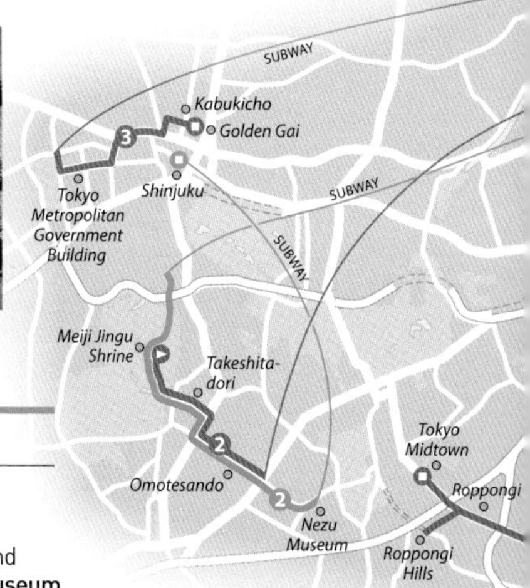

Two Days in Tokyo

Day ❶

MORNING

Take a crash course in art and culture at **Tokyo National Museum** *(see pp24–7)*. Then, stroll around **Ueno Park** *(see pp20–21)* and **Ameyoko Market** *(see p67)*.

AFTERNOON

Enjoy a bird's-eye view of the city from **Tokyo Skytree** *(see p89)* before meandering through Asakusa and the **Senso-ji Temple** complex *(see pp14–15)*. Board the water bus and cruise down the **Sumida River** *(see pp16–17)*. After dark, catch a show at **Kabuki-za Theater** *(see p81)*.

Day ❷

MORNING

Start the day in **Nihonbashi** *(see pp18–19)*, walking over the namesake bridge before heading to the moats, stone walls, and gardens of the grand **Imperial Palace** *(see pp12–13)*. Then, take in the collection at the **National Museum of Modern Art** *(see p12)*.

AFTERNOON

Crunch down the gravel pathway to **Meiji Jingu Shrine** *(see pp30–31)*, and then go shopping on Harajuku's **Takeshita-dori** *(see p56)* and tree-lined **Omotesando** *(see p101)*. The nearby **Nezu Museum** *(see p100)* has a serene garden with a teahouse. In the evening, enjoy the electric vibe of **Shinjuku** *(see pp106–11)*.

Four Days in Tokyo

Day ❶

MORNING

Have breakfast in **Tsukiji Outer Market** *(see p66)*, then tour the **Hamarikyu Garden** *(see p82)*. View the old wooden gates fronting **Zojo-ji Temple** *(see p97)* with the iconic **Tokyo Tower** *(see p96)* in the background.

AFTERNOON

Enjoy the galleries and museums of Roppongi and then browse the shops of **Roppongi Hills** *(see p94)* and **Tokyo Midtown** *(see p95)*, where there are also great places to eat and drink.

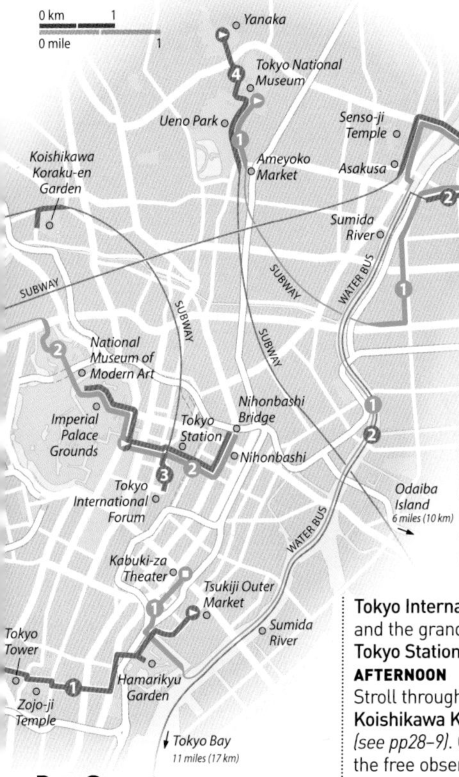

Ueno Park is a green oasis overlooked by modern towers.

Day ❷

MORNING

Pay your respects at **Meiji Jingu Shrine** *(see pp30–31)*, and then browse kitschy stores on **Takeshita-dori** *(see p56)* and high fashion along **Omotesando** *(see p101)*. Cross town for lunch in Asakusa and to explore **Senso-ji Temple** *(see pp14–15)*.

AFTERNOON

Ascend **Tokyo Skytree** *(see p89)* for panoramic views of the city, and then sail into Tokyo Bay on a cruise down the **Sumida River** *(see pp16–17)*.

Day ❸

MORNING

Walk over Nihonbashi Bridge, making your way to the **Imperial Palace** *(see pp12–13)*. After touring the grounds, visit the Marunouchi district, home to the contemporary architecture of the **Tokyo International Forum** *(see p82)* and the grand early 20th-century **Tokyo Station** *(see p76)*.

AFTERNOON

Stroll through the 17th-century **Koishikawa Koraku-en Garden** *(see pp28–9)*. Catch the sunset from the free observation deck of **Tokyo Metropolitan Government Building** *(see p109)* in Shinjuku, and then hit the **Kabukicho** *(see p106)* entertainment area and the warren of drinking dens in **Golden Gai** *(see p107)*.

Day ❹

MORNING

Get acquainted with the shrines, temples, and traditional stores of **Yanaka** *(see pp32–3)*. Afterwards, check out the collection at the **Tokyo National Museum** *(see pp24–7)* and walk around **Ueno Park** *(see pp20–21)*.

AFTERNOON

Ride the train to **Odaiba Island** *(see pp34–5)* to marvel at robot technology at the fascinating **National Museum of Emerging Science and Innovation** *(see p35)*. End your day with some virtual reality fun and games at the **Joypolis** arcade *(see p34)*.

Top 10 Tokyo Highlights

Detail on Senso-ji Temple's elaborate Hozo-mon gateway

Tokyo Highlights 10
Imperial Palace Grounds 12
Senso-ji Temple 14
Sumida River 16
Nihonbashi 18
Ueno Park 20
Tokyo National Museum 24
Koishikawa Koraku-en Garden 28
Meiji Jingu Shrine 30
Yanaka 32
Odaiba Island 34

TOP 10 Tokyo Highlights

The easternmost of the great Asian cities, Tokyo is a city of perpetual change and one that embraces transformation. More interested in the future than the past, it nevertheless carries its history and traditions into the present. This intensely cultural capital is one of the world's most energetic and creative cities. The following 10 sights are a must for any first-time visitor, but there is always something new to discover.

1 Imperial Palace Grounds

Part Forbidden City, part public park, the palace grounds are encircled by moats, stone walls, ancient bridges, keeps, and gardens – elements in the history of the original city *(see pp12–13)*.

2 Senso-ji Temple

The grounds of this temple are packed with attractions, beginning at Kaminari-mon ("Thunder Gate") and the commercial corridor of Nakamise-dori *(see pp14–15)*.

3 Sumida River

An excursion starting under its famous bridges is a journey through the history and development of the city *(see pp16–17)*.

4 Nihonbashi

Packed with centuries-old stores and sleek urban complexes, this district *(see pp18–19)*, set in the heart of Tokyo, is at once traditional and cosmopolitan.

5 Ueno Park

A compendium of Japanese cultural history, this park has mausoleums, temples, museums, a zoo, and a lotus pond. With 1,000 cherry trees, the park is at its best when blossoms are out in spring *(see pp20–21)*.

6 Tokyo National Museum

The world's largest collection of Japanese art and archeology, plus Chinese, Korean, and Central Asian art treasures *(see pp24–7)*.

Koishikawa Koraku-en Garden 7

Tokyo's oldest garden has many features, including a heart-shaped pond and quaint bridges – all rife with symbolism *(see pp28–9)*.

8 Meiji Jingu Shrine

Sited in a forest, the exquisite Shinto architecture of shrine buildings and an iris garden embody the theme of nature *(see pp30–31)*.

Yanaka 9

Set around a leafy cemetery, this neighborhood retains the atmosphere of historic Tokyo, with its temples, shrines, and traditional shopping streets. *(see pp32–3)*.

Odaiba Island 10

With high-tech buildings, exhibition sites, museums, shopping malls, a Ferris wheel, and a beach, the artificial island of Odaiba is a place of entertainment and experiment *(see pp34–5)*.

Imperial Palace Grounds

Located at the center of one of the largest cities in the world, the Imperial Palace grounds sit amid a galaxy of busy urban areas. This enormous compound contains the magnificent residence of the emperor, along with a variety of moats, stone walls, watchtowers, gates, and fairytale bridges. The public areas of the grounds are also home to several museums, galleries, and beautiful Japanese gardens. This is a solemn spot, resonating with cultural meaning, and is among the few places in central Tokyo where one can witness the incredible persistence of history.

1 Sakurada-mon Gate

This entrance to the outer gardens was erected in 1457. A survivor of earthquakes, fires, and air raids, the entrance consists of two structures: one, a broad inner gate, is angled at 90-degrees to thwart intruders.

2 National Museum of Modern Art, Tokyo

More than 12,000 works by Japanese as well as Western artists are exhibited here, dating from the 19th century to the present day. Works include the beautiful *Mother and Child* **(above)** by Shoen Uemura.

3 Ote-mon Gate and Nijubashi Bridge

South of Ote-mon gate, the 1888 reconstructed Nijubashi Bridge **(above)** is a graceful sight. The bridge is a popular backdrop for photos.

4 Imperial Palace East Gardens

Designed by Kobori Enshu in the early 17th century, these gardens **(right)** feature stone lanterns, bridges, ponds, swathes of flowers, and towering zelkova trees.

5 Shiomizaka

Stone walls line the path up to the "Tide View Slope." The small promontory once commanded fine views of the sea and Mount Fuji.

6 Imperial Palace Plaza

The plaza's pristine lawns, cherry trees, and stands of ornamental black pines were laid out in 1899. The gravel concourse acts as a firebreak. The plaza offers lovely views of Nijubashi Bridge.

Imperial Palace Grounds

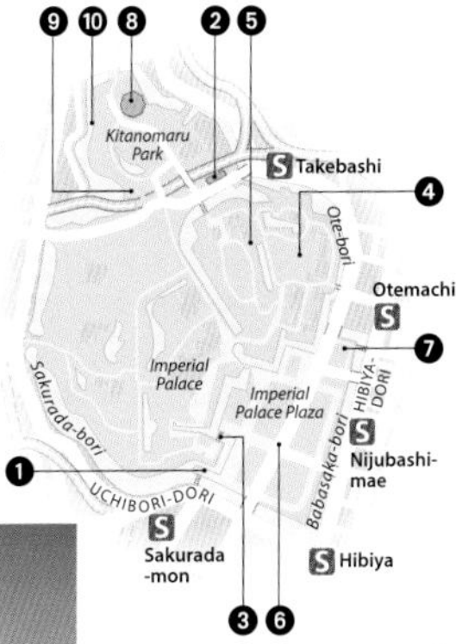

TRAUMAS IN THE GARDENS

The tranquil gardens of today's palace grounds have known their fair share of drama. Victims of the great 1923 earthquake sheltered here. During the war, several members of Japan's officer corps, inconsolable at news of their nation's defeat, came here in August 1945 to commit ritual suicide. In the 1950s and 1960s, the plaza witnessed violent political demonstrations.

8 Nippon Budokan

The colossal octagonal roof of the Budokan, or Japan Martial Arts Hall, features onion-shaped finials covered in gold leaf. Its elements mirror those seen in traditional Japanese temples.

9 Sannomaru Shozokan

Located within the East Garden, this small museum displays art, artifacts, calligraphy, and other items connected to the imperial family.

7 Wadakura Fountain Park

This striking aquatic park was built in 1961 to commemorate the wedding of the present emperor's parents. The fountains are illuminated in the evening.

10 Chidorigafuchi

The stone walls of the shogun's former castle contrast with the inky waters of Chidorigafuchi moat **(above)**, which is home to turtles, carp, cormorants, egrets, and gliding swans.

NEED TO KNOW

MAP K1–M4 ■ 1-1 Chiyoda, Chiyoda ■ sankan.kunaicho.go.jp/english

Adm for museums and galleries

■ All museums in the complex are closed on Mondays (except for public holidays). Visit the grounds early: the tour groups turn up by mid-morning. Late February is the best season to see plum blossoms and early April for cherry blossoms, while azaleas and dogwood flowers bloom in mid-May.

■ Have a picnic in Kitanomaru Park, or head south of the palace for Hibiya Park, where café Hibiya Saroh serves noodles and sandwiches.

Senso-ji Temple

Rebuilt countless times since its founding in 628, the spectacular Senso-ji Temple is the oldest temple site in Tokyo. The current temple, dedicated to Kannon, the Goddess of Mercy, is a fireproof replica of an earlier version built in 1692. One of the liveliest spots in the city, its grounds attract throngs of visitors, who come to pray inside its cavernous main hall with its opulent, golden altar and priceless collection of 18th- and 19th-century votive paintings. This religious sanctuary lies at the heart of a busy commercial and entertainment district.

1 Kaminari-mon Gate

This giant gate is flanked by two gods: Fujin and Raijin. A red paper lantern with the characters for "thunder gate" emblazoned on it hangs within **(above)**.

2 Incense Burner

A giant bronze incense burner **(above)** stands in front of the main hall. The faithful burn pink sticks of incense, wafting the smoke over their clothes for good luck.

3 Niten-mon Gate

Designated an Important Cultural Treasure, the ox-blood-colored gate to the east dates from 1618. Its pillars and walls are covered with votive papers stuck there by the faithful.

4 Giant Straw Sandals

Two large straw sandals hang on the Hozo-mon Gate. Made for deities with feet of mythic size, they symbolize the traditional footwear of the Buddhist pilgrim.

5 Nakamise-dori

The main avenue to the city's holiest sanctuary is packed with more than 150 stalls and booths selling traditional goods and souvenirs.

NEED TO KNOW

MAP R2 ■ 2-3-1 Asakusa, Taito ■ www.senso-ji.jp

Open 24 hrs daily

Denbo-in Garden: open mid-Mar–early May

■ Get there early to avoid the crowds.

■ Combine a trip to the temple with a cruise on the Sumida River from Azuma Bridge.

■ Grab a table outside at one of the many local restaurants to the west of the temple for lunch or dinner.

6 Senso-ji Main Hall

Senso-ji Temple's main hall **(below)** has a lavish interior, the centerpiece of which is a richly decorated gold and lacquer altar. Walls have votive paintings and the ceiling has a colorful dragon motif surrounded by angels and lotuses.

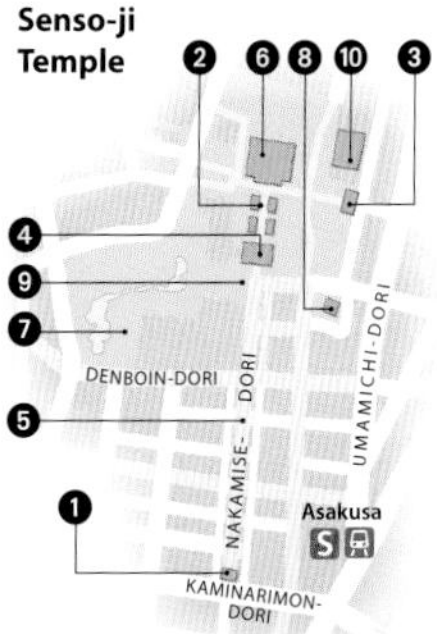

7 Denbo-in Garden

This tranquil garden **(below)** was designed in the early 1600s by the Zen gardener Kobori Enshu. Tea ceremonies are performed in a small pavilion beside the pond.

8 Benten Mound

Dedicated to Benten, goddess of beauty and the arts, a red shrine sits atop a hill built over an ancient burial mound. A bell rings for the opening of the temple grounds.

MYSTERY OF THE GOLDEN KANNON

On March 18, 628, two fishermen brothers found a golden statue of the goddess Kannon in their nets. The 2-inch (5-cm) image is today enshrined in the Senso-ji Temple. Upon the moment of its discovery, according to legend, a golden dragon danced from heaven to earth. A Golden Dragon Dance is held in the temple grounds every spring and fall to mark the occasion.

9 Nade Jizo

This bronze bodhisattva statue **(above)**, a figure of compassion, is believed to relieve ailments if you rub the part of its body that troubles you.

10 Asakusa Jinja

At the entrance to the 1649 shrine's main hall sit protective lion-dog statues **(above)**, which honor two brothers who found an image of the goddess Kannon in their fishing nets.

TOP 10 Sumida River

The Sumida River, Tokyo's premier waterway, has long been a symbol of the city. While its water and embankments are a setting for commerce, festivals, gardens, bridges, and ferries, its literary associations form a rich body of lore. The girders, shackles, and bolts of older bridges, with their sweeping arches, stone stanchions, and wrought-iron lanterns, lend a sense of continuity to the everchanging Tokyo. Low-hulled sculls operated by oarsmen have now given way to waterbuses and pleasure boats.

1 Kiyosu Bridge

Built in 1928, this blue bridge **(above)** was inspired by one that once crossed the Rhine in Cologne. Its eight lanterns are lit at twilight.

2 Asahi Beer Hall

Set above Azuma Bridge, this striking black building **(above)**, designed by Philippe Starck, is in the form of an inverted pyramid. Even more surreal is the rooftop installation known as the *Flamme d'Or*.

3 Tsukuda-jima

The first residents of this island congregated at Sumiyoshi Shrine, which is dedicated to Sumiyoshi Myojin, protector of seafarers.

4 Yanagi Bridge

Featured in many *ukiyo-e* prints, this green bridge dates back to the Edo era. It stands at the heart of an old geisha district, marking the boundary between Chuo Ward to the south and Taito Ward to the north. Houseboats and fishing boats are moored here.

5 Komagata Bridge

The curving blue girders and stone stanchions of this bridge, built in 1927, combine strength and elegance. The span's eight lanterns are lit at twilight, creating one of the city's most romantic nighttime scenes.

6 Eitai Bridge

Convicts were once loaded onto boats from this bridge **(above)** and shipped off to Japan's penal colonies. It offers sweeping scenic river views.

7 Basho Inari Shrine and Statue

Dedicated to the haiku poet Matsuo Basho (1644–94), this shrine leads to an elevated garden with a seated statue of him.

8 Hamarikyu Garden

Features of the original garden can be seen in the tidal pond, in islets linked by wooden bridges, and in a tea pavilion. The pond is home to saltwater fish.

NEED TO KNOW

Asakusa Pier: **MAP R2**

Hamarikyu Pier: **MAP N6**

- The best way to see the river highlights is to take a water bus *(see p123)* between Asakusa and Hamarikyu Garden, or a little farther on to Odaiba Island. Enthusiasts of the poet Basho can stroll just north of the Basho Inari Shrine to the Basho Memorial Hall, a research center with manuscripts, calligraphy, and illustrations of scenes from his life.
- Near Ryogoku JR station, Popeye is a great place for German- and Japanese-style snacks and craft beer.

RIVER FIREWORKS

Since 1732, the Sumida River around Asakusa has hosted spectacular firework displays. On the last Saturday of July, tens of thousands of pyrotechnic wonders illuminate the night sky between the Sakura and Umaya bridges. Arrive early to secure prime view spots, as the festival attracts around one million spectators.Better yet, book a cruise on a boat for an unbeatable view of the illuminations from the water.

9 Umaya Bridge

This imposing steel structure is named after the shogun's horse stables, once located west of the bridge. Bas-relief horses appear on the ornamental pillars.

10 Tokyo Skytree

The world's tallest free-standing tower has observation decks at two levels, along with a restaurant. It dazzles most when illuminated at night **(above)**.

TOP 10 Nihonbashi

Located in the heart of central Tokyo, Nihonbashi – named after its famous namesake bridge – has been a thriving commercial center since the early Edo era. It is home to many of the capital's oldest and most respected businesses, including department stores, financial institutions, and specialist craft shops. Today, it mixes these traditional businesses with sleek skyscrapers, modern complexes, luxury hotels, and trendy bars and restaurants. No other place in Tokyo blends the historic and contemporary quite as effortlessly as Nihonbashi.

1 Nihonbashi Bridge

Built in 1603 as a wooden bridge, with the iconic stone version **(right)** erected in 1911, this is where the five highways connecting Kyoto and Edo all started. A plaque in the center of the bridge marks the point from where all distances from Tokyo are measured.

2 Mitsukoshi

Founded in 1673 as a kimono shop, Mitsukoshi has since morphed into one of Japan's classic department stores.

3 Currency Museum

Run by the neighboring Bank of Japan, this entry free museum traces the development of Japanese and east Asian currencies, with a collection stretching from Edo-era gold ingots to pre-World War II banknotes.

4 Canal Cruises

From a jetty near Nihonbashi Bridge, boats **(right)** head off on short tours exploring Tokyo Bay and the city's old waterways. These canals were once vital trade routes, but now offer an alternate view of the city.

5 Takashimaya

One of Japan's best-known department stores, Takashimaya is worth a look for its fusion of Western and traditional Japanese architecture. Don't miss the impressive food hall in the basement.

6 Mitsui Memorial Museum

Showcasing the collection of one of Japan's most influential business families, the Mitsuis, this museum focuses on Japanese and east Asian art and artifacts from the Edo era onwards.

7 Haibara

The historic Haibara has been selling *washi* (traditional handmade paper) since 1806. You'll find a variety of sheet *washi*, and also *washi*-made boxes and pen stands.

8 Coredo Muromachi

Spread over three buildings, this swanky complex **(left)** is home to an excellent selection of craft stores, fashion and interior design boutiques, restaurants, bars, and traditional delis. There's also a tea ceremony center and a cinema.

9 Koami Shrine

Established in 1466 to ward off the plague, this shrine **(above)** now draws visitors for a very different reason. Rinsing money in the shrine's water basin is said to bring wealth and prosperity.

10 Tokyo Stock Exchange

A reminder of Nihonbashi's financial clout, the TSE is one of the world's most important stock exchanges. Tours offer a glimpse of the trading floor in action.

NEED TO KNOW

MAP N1–P1

Mitsukoshi: 1-4-1 Nihonbashimuromachi; open 10am–7pm daily (restaurants 11am–10pm); www.mistore.jp/store/nihombashi

Currency Museum: 1-3-1 Nihonbashihongokucho, Chuo; open 9:30am–4:30pm Tue–Sun; www.imes.boj.or.jp/cm/english

Canal Cruises: 1-9 Nihonbashi, Chuo; times vary, see website; www.nihonbashi-cruise.jp

Takashimaya: 2-4-1 Nihonbashi, Chuo; open 10:30am–7:30pm daily (restaurants to 9pm); www.takashimaya.co.jp

Mitsui Memorial Museum: 2-1-1 Nihonbashimuromachi, Chuo; open 11am–4pm Tue–Sun; adm; www.mitsui-museum.jp

Haibara: 2-7-1 Nihonbashi, Chuo; open 10am–6:30pm Mon–Fri (to 5:30pm Sat & Sun); www.haibara.co.jp/en

Coredo Muromachi: 2-2-1 Nihonbashimuromachi; open 11am–8pm daily (bars and restaurants to 11pm); www.mitsui-shopping-park.com/urban/muromachi

Tokyo Stock Exchange: 2-1 Nihonbashikabutocho, Chuo; self-guided tours 9:30am–4:30pm Mon–Fri; www.jpx.co.jp/english

- **During cherry blossom season, Nihonbashi celebrates the flowering of sakura with events, including light shows.**
- **Take a detour to Ningyocho for its craft stores and confectioners.**

Ueno Park

Home to one of the most impressive concentrations of high art in the city, Ueno Park sits at the center of a down-to-earth residential and entertainment district. With its temples, shrines, cherry trees, a magnificent lotus pond, statues, and tombs, the park is like a miniature model of Japan. The hill, on which the upper part of the park sits, was once a great religious center. During the Meiji and Taisho periods, this historical stage served as a venue for large-scale art and industrial exhibitions, paving the way for the venerable museums and galleries that occupy the park today. Huge numbers gather here during the spring cherry-blossom season.

1 Ueno Zoo

Built in 1882, this zoo is home to Indian lions, Sumatran tigers, giant pandas, and other critters. A monorail ride leads to a tamer petting section.

2 Toshogu Shrine and Kara-mon Gate

This opulent shrine **(right)**, dedicated to the first shogun, Tokugawa Ieyasu, was built in 1627. A row of stone and copper lanterns leads to the shrine.

NEED TO KNOW

MAP F1–F2
■ Uenokoen, Taito

Open 24 hrs daily

■ **Those interested in art can combine a visit to the park with a trip to the Taikan Yokoyama Memorial Hall, the painter's private house, which stands opposite Shinobazu Pond.**

■ **The causeway leading from the large *torii* (gate) to Benten island is lined with food stalls. This is a great place to try traditional snacks and light dishes.**

3 National Museum of Western Art

Designed by Le Corbusier, the museum's exhibits range from 15th-century religious pieces to works by Pollock and Miro.

4 Gojo Tenjin and Hanazono Inari Fox Shrines

Winding paths lead through red *torii* (gates) **(right)** to Hanazono and Gojo shrines. Inari fox statues stand inside.

5 Cherry Trees

In spring, the park's cherry blossoms **(above)** attract large crowds for *hanami* (flower viewing) parties, complete with sake, beer, and karaoke.

> **MEIJI RESTORATION**
>
> A fierce battle between supporters of the deposed shogun and the new forces of the Meiji restoration was fought on Ueno Hill in 1868. Heavy rains flooded Shinobazu Pond, with men combating in knee-deep water, while a cannon shot from a teahouse on one side of the water and another from a cave dedicated to Inari exploded over their heads. Over 300 men died in the conflict.

9 Benten-do

This temple honors the Goddess of Beauty **(left)**. The ceiling inside the hall is painted with dragons, and the walls with murals of fall flowers.

10 Shinobazu Pond

The pond's southern section is filled with pink lotuses during the summer. Reeds provide a habitat for herons, grebes, and thousands of other water fowl.

6 Saigo Takamori Statue

The bronze statue, unveiled in 1898, is a tribute to Takamori, a powerful samurai who led a major rebellion in the 19th century. He is shown wearing a summer kimono, walking his dog.

7 Five-Story Pagoda

Covered with bronze roof tiles to protect it from fire, the current pagoda was built in 1640. The 120-ft- (37-m-) tall vermillion structure is located inside the zoo.

8 Shitamachi Museum

Displaying a range of everyday items such as kitchenware, tools, and furniture, this museum also features re-creations of Edo-era stores and tenements.

Ueno Park

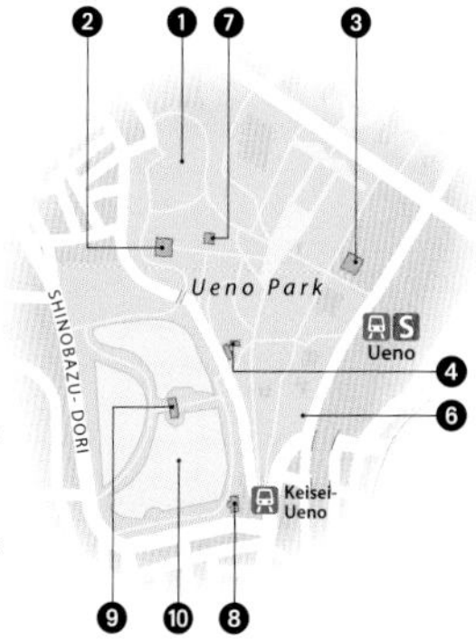

Tokyo National Museum

Occupying a major part of the northern reaches of Ueno Park, the colossal Tokyo National Museum was known in the prewar period as the Imperial Household Museum. This magisterial museum, set among courtyards, fountains, and trees, is divided into four main galleries: Honkan, Heiseikan, Toyokan, and Gallery of Horyu-ji Treasures. These contain not only the most important collection of Japanese art and archeology in the world, but a treasure trove of Asian antiquities as well. The main galleries display almost 4,000 items at any one time – a huge amount to see in one visit. There is a garden on the side of the Honkan which opens for the cherry blossom and fall foliage seasons.

1 Japanese Paintings and Prints

The Honkan features paintings from the classical Heian to Muromachi periods, as well as fine examples of mural, screen, and paper door art, and Zen-inspired ink landscapes. The highlight of the Edo era is the work of its *ukiyo-e* woodblock print artists **(right)**.

2 Ceramics

Japanese ceramics **(above)** in the Honkan are represented by Kyoto and Imari ware. The Toyokan has Chinese ceramics from the Song to Qing dynasties.

3 Lacquerware

Included among the Japanese National Treasures and Important Cultural Properties exhibited in the Honkan are stunning *maki-e* lacquerware items dating from the Heian to Edo periods.

4 The Gallery of Horyu-ji Treasures

This gallery displays an invaluable collection of more than 300 objects from Horyu-ji Temple in Nara, including a forest of standing bodhisattvas.

Previous pages *Cherry trees in full bloom at Ueno Park*

5 Japanese Archeology

The Heiseikan, dedicated to Japanese archeology, houses relics from the Jomon period (c.14,000–300 BC) onward. The chronology of Japanese arts can be found here.

6 Asian Arts

The Toyokan is the gallery to see Asian art. The collection includes fine examples of Korean metalwork, Khmer pottery, Hindu statuary, and cave paintings from the grottoes of Bingling, China.

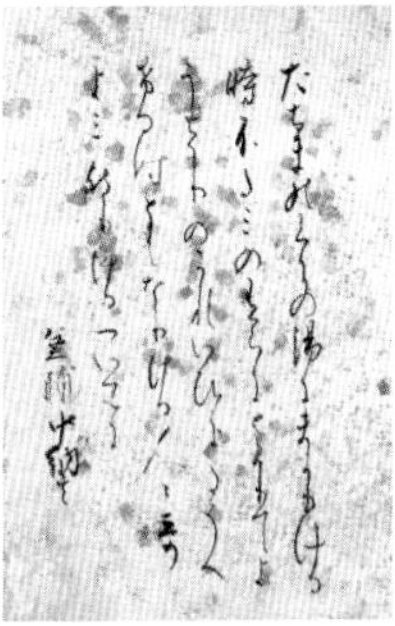

7 Calligraphy

The master calligraphy in the Honkan includes *bokuseki*, executed by Zen priests **(above)**. Even if the meanings of the Chinese characters elude you, the beauty of the brushwork will not.

8 Textiles

The Toyokan has a sumptuous collection of textiles from China, Korea, Southeast Asia, Central Asia, India, and Egypt. The exquisite Indonesian brocade work made from gold thread can also be seen here **(left)**. The Honkan houses Japanese textiles.

9 Arms and Armor

The equipment once owned by Japan's military elite is displayed in the Honkan. Often excessively embellished, this includes the warriors' attire: armor, helmets, saddlery, and sword mountings.

10 Religious Sculptures

Religious sculptures **(left)** are scattered throughout the galleries. Bronze, gilt, and sandstone sculptures from Pakistan are exhibited in the Toyokan. The Honkan displays Buddhist statues from India and Japan.

NEED TO KNOW

MAP F1 ■ Uenokoen, Taito ■ 3822-1111 ■ www.tnm.jp

Open 9:30am–5pm Tue–Sun

Adm

■ **The museum shop on the first floor of the Honkan gallery sells beautiful items linked to the museum's exhibits and motifs.**

■ **The Hotel Okura Garden terrace in The Gallery of Horyu-ji is a pleasant setting for lunch. There are cheaper options at the stalls and cafés in Ueno Park.**

Museum Guide

The main gate to the museum complex, which consists of four major galleries, lies at the north end of Ueno Park. The central gallery, the Honkan, is straight ahead, beyond the pond. The Toyokan is on the right, and the Heiseikan is to the left, behind the Honkan. The Gallery of Horyu-ji Treasures lies to the left of the main gate, behind the Hyokeikan, a grand building open only for special exhibits and events.

Galleries and Outdoor Features

Exterior of the Honkan, which contains Japanese art and artifacts

1 Honkan

The main gallery and centerpiece of Ueno Park was designed by Jin Watanabe. The present Honkan was built in 1938 in the "Imperial Crown" style of architecture. The features are Japanese, but the building materials are undeniably Western.

2 Toyokan

Asian artworks and archeological exhibits are housed in a light, modernist building. Parts of the collection may sometimes be shown elsewhere within the complex.

Teahouse in the museum garden

3 Museum Garden and Teahouses

The site is open to the public during the spring cherry-blossom or fall leaf-viewing seasons. Those who are in Tokyo around this time should not pass up the chance to see the secret pond-garden and teahouses on the north side of the Honkan.

4 Heiseikan

Opened in 1993 – with a sleek courtyard, auditorium, and lounge – this modern gallery houses pottery, burial statues, and artifacts from the ancient world.

5 Research and Information Center

Built in 1984, this center lets visitors browse through archives, books, magazines, monochrome and color photographs, and other materials linked to art history.

6 Gallery of Horyu-ji Treasures

The minimalist 1999 design of this gallery is the work of Yoshio Taniguchi, whose overseas projects include the groundbreaking Museum of Modern Art (MOMA) in New York.

7 Black Gate

A rare structure from the Edo period, the Kuro-mon is topped with a heavy hip-and-gable style roof. Old roof tiles and foundation stones are kept in the rear of the gate.

8 Azekura Sutra Store

Buddhist sutras were once kept in stores like this one, transported in 1882 from Gango-ji Temple in Nara. Constructed of logs, the

ASIAN ART THEMES

With over 110,000 objects in its collection, the Tokyo National Museum regularly rotates its exhibits. The Tokyokan consists of 13 exhibition rooms divided by regional themes. The themes listed opposite at the Toyokan are part of its permanent collection, but individual displays change.

This Gandharan sculpture is one of the highlights of the collection housed in the Toyokan.

STONE AGE TOKYO

Early settlers lived along the ridges and bluffs of the present-day Yamanote Hills. From here, they had ready access to plentiful supplies of fish and shellfish. A pre-Bronze Age site – the Omori shell mound – in southwest Tokyo was discovered in 1877 by the American zoologist Edward Sylvester Morse. The event marked the beginning of Japanese archeology.

TOP 10 ASIAN ART THEMES

1 Indian and Gandharan Sculpture (13th–2nd century BC)

2 Ancient Asian Bronze Drums (6th–5th century BC)

3 West Asian Textiles (19th century)

4 Chinese Archeology (2nd–1st century BC)

5 Chinese Textiles (15th–17th century)

6 Chinese Ceramics (Three Kingdoms period–Tang dynasty)

7 Chinese Ceramics (Song–Qing dynasty)

8 Chinese Stone Reliefs from Shangdong (1st–2nd century)

9 Korean Ceramics (9th–10th century)

10 Khmer Sculptures (Angkor period)

inner walls of this tiny storehouse are decorated with murals depicting bodhisattvas and protective deities.

9 Hyokeikan

A prized example of a Meiji-era Western-style building, the white stone walls and green domes of this Important Cultural Property are an impressive if somewhat sober sight.

10 Statue of Edward Jenner

British physician Edward Jenner (1749–1823) was the pioneer of vaccination. This memorial statue by Unkai Yonehara, a pupil of sculptor Koun Takamura, was erected in 1896 as a tribute to Jenner and his great achievement.

The Hyokeikan, built in 1909

Koishikawa Koraku-en Garden

Established in 1629, Tokyo's oldest surviving garden was commissioned by Yorifusa Tokugawa, lord of the Mito branch of the Tokugawa family. Its designer, Tokudaiji Sahei, was aided by the Confucian scholar, Zhu Shunshui, a Chinese refugee from the fall of the Ming dynasty. The garden was once a recreational space for the Tokugawa clan to entertain guests, clamber up its miniature hills, float in barges on its pond, and stage poetry parties.

1 Mount Lu and Lotuses

Miniature landscapes here recall famous places in poetry and mythology. Below this imitation of Mount Lu in China **(above)** is a sacred lotus pond.

NEED TO KNOW

MAP E2 ■ 1-6-6 Koraku, Bunkyo ■ 3811-3015 ■ www.tokyo-park.or.jp/teien/en/koishikawa

Open 9am–5pm daily

Adm

■ **Try to get to the garden when it opens, before the amusement park next door gets into full swing. In the fierce summer months the garden is much cooler than its surroundings.**

■ **Kantoku-tei, a teahouse with a room facing onto Oigawa pond, serves *matcha* (powdered green tea) along with a traditional Japanese confection.**

2 Horai-jima Island

The island located at the pond's center represents the Taoist paradise of Horai-jima. The idea of a "heavenly isle" in a garden was conceived by the Chinese Emperor Wu.

3 Engetsukyo Bridge

A stroll along the winding, tree-sheltered paths leads to the Chinese-style Engetsukyo **(below)**, the "round moon bridge," arguably the oldest ornamental stone bridge in Tokyo.

4 Tsuiji Walls

The current wall is a reinforced concrete imitation of the original *tsuiji* plastered walls, but moss and staining from Tokyo's steamy summers have given the newer walls a patina of age.

5 Symbolic Rice Field

Created to show the hardships faced by peasant farmers, a rice field lies to the north of the garden. School kids plant and harvest the crop.

6 Kuhachiya House

Standing in the middle of a glade of red pines, this thatched-roof building is modeled on an Edo-era drinking house.

7 Tsutenkyo Bridge

Spanning a deep ravine and supported on piles, the bridge **(above)** is a replica of a structure in Kyoto's Tofuku-ji Temple. Its reflection in the shallow river amplifies its size.

8 Iris Garden

Planted in the marsh surrounding the zigzag bridge, purple and white Japanese and rabbit-ear irises bloom during the June rainy season. An ancient system of sluice gates and dikes irrigates the marsh.

Koishikawa Koraku-en Garden

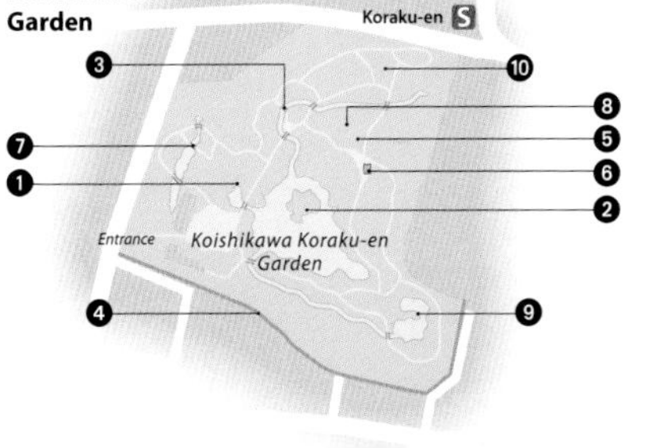

JAPANESE TEA CEREMONY

The dual purpose of the ceremony is to create a spirit of modesty and to express deep hospitality among tea guests. Stepping stones leading to the teahouse are designed to slow down guests, to decrease the pace of ordinary life. The very low entrance requires guests to stoop, a gesture of humility that places everyone on an equal social footing.

9 Inner Garden

Apart from a long-gone Chinese gate, everything else remains the same as when the Mito family used this Chinese-style inner garden as a sanctum and place of study.

10 Plum Orchard and Yatsu-hashi

An attractive plum orchard **(above)** just to the north of the pond comes into fragrant white blossom in early February. Nearby, a zigzag, eight-span *yatsu-hashi* bridge runs through a small marsh.

Meiji Jingu Shrine

Dedicated to the memory of Emperor Meiji (1852–1912) and his wife, Empress Shoken, Meiji Jingu Shrine is a fine example of restrained Shinto architecture. Completed in 1921, the shrine was destroyed in an air raid in 1945. The current reconstruction is indistinguishable from the original. The gravel paths and courtyards of the grounds host cultural events, ranging from Noh and Kyogen drama, court dances, and music performances to horseback archery, winter ice sculptures, and calligraphy shows.

1 Torii

The 39-ft (12-m) main gate **(above)** is Japan's largest *torii*, constructed from 1,500-year-old Japanese *hinoki* cypress trees. It marks the entrance to the shrine's evergreen forest.

2 Ichi no Torii

Meaning "first gate," this *torii* is positioned at the main entrance to Meiji Jingu Shrine. *Torii* symbolize the perch where a mythological cock sat before it announced the dawn that lured the sun goddess Amaterasu from her cave. The 16-petal chrysanthemum medallions at the top of the gate are a symbol of the imperial family.

3 Main Shrine

This elegant and classic Shinto-style shrine **(right)** can be entered through one of three decorated, wooden gates.

4 Meiji Jingu Museum

Opened in 2019 and designed by prominent Japanese architect Kengo Kuma, this museum is set in a large woodland. It houses items connected to Emperor Meiji and Empress Shokan, including an ornately decorated imperial carriage.

NEED TO KNOW

MAP B5 ■ 1-1 Yoyogi Kamizonocho, Shibuya ■ 3379-5511 ■ www.meijijingu.or.jp/en

Main Shrine: open dawn to dusk

Iris Garden: open 9am–4pm (to 4:30pm Mar–Oct); adm

Meiji Jingu Museum: open 9am–4:30pm Fri–Wed; adm

■ The shrine is at its busiest on *hatsumode*, on 1 January, when people come here to make wishes for the new year.

■ The boundary of adjacent Yoyogi Park *(see p51)* has stalls selling snacks, light meals, and other refreshments.

EMPEROR MEIJI

In 1867, two British emissaries, Sir Harry Parkes and Algernon Mitford, were granted an audience with the 15-year-old emperor in his palace in Kyoto. What they found was a vision of medieval sovereignty: a boy dressed in white brocade and silk trousers, his teeth lacquered black, eyebrows shaved, and cheeks painted red. Less than a year later, he would proclaim the Meiji era and by the end of his reign, Japan was an industrialized nation, strong enough to have defeated Russia in 1904–5.

5 Votive Tablets

Hung on prayer boards in front of the shrine **(right)**, *ema* (votive tablets sending prayers to the god) are still popular, especially among students petitioning for divine help in passing exams. Another *ema* is usually hung in gratitude, if a wish is fulfilled.

8 JR Bridge

The bridge leading to the shrine is a free zone for performance artists, some of whom enjoy dressing up in rococo hairstyles and gothic makeup.

6 Traditional Wedding Processions

Along with the many other rituals and dedicatory ceremonies held at the shrine, Shinto weddings **(above)** are quietly formal in manner and attire, but visually dazzling. Most weddings take place on Saturday afternoons.

7 Evergreen Forest

Much of the grounds are densely forested. More than 120,000 trees and shrubs form a natural garden of Japanese flora.

9 Souvenir Store

Amulets, incense, talismans, lucky arrows, key rings strung with a tiny shrine bell, and models of tanuki (raccoon-dog deity) are sold here.

10 Meiji Jingu Shrine Iris Garden

A wooded path leads into a sunken garden **(below)**, bordered by misty woods and thatched gazebos. In early June, purple, pink, and white irises bloom in the water garden.

TOP 10 Yanaka

An oasis of calm, seemingly frozen in time, Yanaka is a far cry from the idea of Tokyo as a metropolis of the future. The area, a short stroll north of Ueno Park but more easily accessed from Nippori Station on the JR Yamanote line, is where some 60 temples and shrines relocated after a fire devastated the city's downtown area in 1657. They remain there today alongside the elegiac Yanaka Cemetery, the last resting place of many of the city's luminaries, and Yanaka Ginza, a traditional shopping street straight out of Tokyo's past.

1 Yanaka Ginza

Global chains are banished from this shopping street in favor of stores selling meat and groceries, cafés **(above)**, *soba* restaurants, and crafts stores such as Yanaka Matsunoya, which sells artisan-made household goods.

2 Suwa Shrine

At New Year, the grounds of this 1202 shrine on the edge of a plateau are strung with lanterns showing the animal zodiac sign for the coming year.

3 Zensho-an Temple

Every August, this Zen temple displays its collection of painted scrolls depicting supernatural folk tales.

4 Kotozan Daien-ji Temple

This temple has a Buddhist and a Shinto hall. Its Chrysanthemum Festival is held here annually on October 14–15, when dolls made from flowers are displayed and puppet performances take place.

5 Yanaka Cemetery

The graves of the last shogun **(above)**, Yoshinobu Tokugawa (1837-1913), and the infamous murderess Takahashi Oden are among the many notable figures buried in this cemetery.

6 Tenno-ji Temple

Founded in 1274, this temple contains the Great Buddha of Yanaka **(above)**, a fine bronze statue cast in 1690.

8 Isetatsu

This 1864 shop **(left)** creates *chiyogami* – patterned *washi* (Japanese handmade paper) once popular with the samurai class. Today, the paper is used for decorative purposes and origami.

7 Ueno Sakuragi Atari

Get a glimpse of life in the Edo period: three traditional wooden houses built in 1938 have been converted into a brewpub, a bakery, two stores, and a community space.

9 SCAI – The Bathhouse

Located in a renovated 200-year-old former bathhouse, this gallery focuses on contemporary art. The works of modern icons like Tatsuo Miyajima are displayed here.

GREAT BUDDHA OF YANAKA

Yanaka locals have a special affection for their very own Great Buddha of Yanaka. The 16-ft (5-m) statue belongs to Tenno-ji Temple, a sanctuary that was damaged during the Battle of Ueno (1868) *(see p21)*. The fact that the statue survived added to its mystic appeal. Cast in bronze in 1690, this Chinese-style figure has finely carved facial features, representing the Shaka-nyorai Buddha. It stands in a tranquil corner of the temple precincts, among lush surroundings.

10 Asakura Museum of Sculpture

The former home and studio of sculptor Fumio Asakura (1883–1964) contains many of his graceful statues.

Yanaka

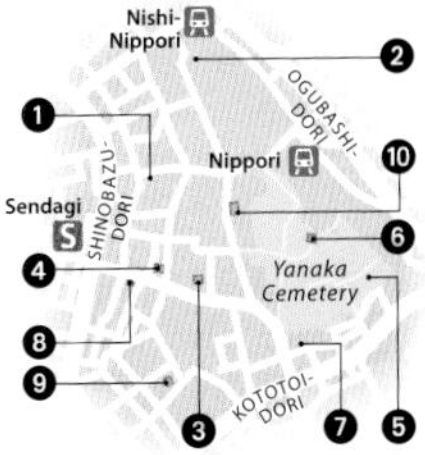

NEED TO KNOW

MAP F1

Ueno Sakuragi Atari: opening times vary, check website for details; www.uenosakuragiatari.jp

Isetatsu: open 10am–6pm; www.isetatsu.com

SCAI – The Bathhouse: 3821-1144; open noon–6pm Tue–Sat; www.scaithebathhouse.com

Asakura Museum of Sculpture: 3821-4549; open 9:30am–4:30pm Tue–Wed, Fri–Sun; adm

■ Yanaka is full of free art galleries. Drop by Haco *(6-1-27 Yanaka; www.haco-yanaka.com)*, which displays art and crafts by up-and-coming local artists. Another great gallery is Art Sanctuary *(1-6-17 Yanaka; www.allanwest.jp)*, the studio of American artist Allan West, who is well-known for making gilded screens and scrolls inspired by nature.

Odaiba Island

When coastal megacities run out of space, they inevitably turn toward the sea. An aerial view of Tokyo reveals a city stretched to its limits, coming to a congested stop at the waterfront. Geometrically precise islands appear, seemingly lowered into place like space panels. As well as the exhibition pavilions, indoor shopping malls, game centers, cafés, restaurants, and surrealistic constructions of Odaiba Island, visitors are intrigued by the structures on this landfill that seem to hail from the future rather than the past.

1 Rainbow Bridge

At night, this graceful bridge **(above)** is illuminated and in summer fireworks displays are held on the waters around the bridge's stanchions.

DEFENDING THE BAY

The Edo-era Tokugawa government built artificial islands as cannon batteries to protect Tokyo from foreign invasion. The fear was well founded. In the 1850s, heavily armed American steamships, led by Commodore Perry, moored close offshore *(see p38)*. In all, six islands were built. However, only Battery Island Nos. 3 and 6 remain today.

2 Tyffonium

Immersive, cutting-edge virtual reality (VR) attractions, such as a walk-through house of horrors and a fantastical world full of ghost ships, are the main draw of this amusement center.

3 RiSuPia

Electronics giant Panasonic shows off its latest gadgets and has a great hands-on science and discovery center, which is a fun distraction for kids and adults.

4 Joypolis

This popular indoor amusement park **(below)** has the latest arcade machines, some of the city's most exciting VR experiences, including zombie laser tag, and an interactive roller coaster.

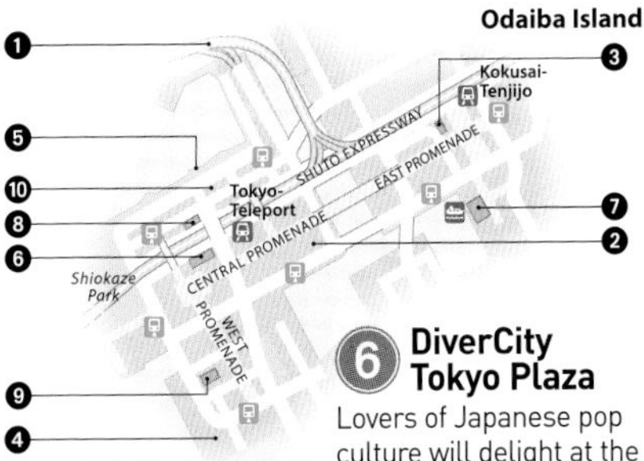

5 Odaiba Marine Park

An artificial beach and a replica of New York's Statue of Liberty are among the attractions of this park, along with mesmerizing views of the city skyline and Rainbow Bridge.

6 DiverCity Tokyo Plaza

Lovers of Japanese pop culture will delight at the statue of the anime robot Gundam in front of this mega-shopping mall, which has a Gundam-themed exhibition hall.

7 Tokyo Big Sight

The megalithic exhibition center has an eighth-floor observation space. The gravity-defying structure consists of four inverted pyramids standing on a seemingly narrow base.

8 Fuji TV Building

Two blocks of this Kenzo Tange-designed building **(above)** are joined by girder-like sky corridors and a titanium-paneled sphere. The Observation Deck offers the finest view of Tokyo.

9 National Museum of Emerging Science and Innovation

Laid out in a futuristic building, this museum focuses on space, life sciences, and cutting-edge technology **(below)**.

10 Decks Tokyo Beach

This sprawling mall has many outdoor patios and restaurants, as well as fun attractions such as a small LEGOLAND® and Madame Tussauds™.

NEED TO KNOW

MAP D2

Tyffonium: opening times vary, see website; adm; www.tyffonium.com

RiSuPia: 3599-2600; open 10am–6pm Tue–Sun; adm

Joypolis: opening times vary, see website; www.tokyo-joypolis.com; adm

National Museum of Emerging Science and Innovation: open 10am–5pm Wed–Mon; adm; www.miraikan.jst.go.jp/en

Tokyo Big Sight: www.bigsight.jp/english

Fuji TV Building: open 10am–6pm Tue–Sun; adm; www.fujitv.com/visit_fujitv

DiverCity Tokyo Plaza: 6380-7800; opening times vary, see website; mitsui-shopping-park.com/divercity-tokyo

- **The island gets packed on weekends.**
- **Dine at the food theme park of Odaiba Takoyaki Museum in the Decks mall.**

The Top 10 of Everything

Moments in History	**38**
Historic Buildings	**40**
Places of Worship	**42**

Shinjuku Gyoen Garden in fall

Museums	44
Art Galleries	46
Modern and Contemporary Buildings	48
Gardens and Parks	50
Off the Beaten Path	52
Children's Attractions	54
Pop Culture Venues	56
Entertainment Venues	58
Onsen and Sento	60
Restaurants	62
Cafés and Bars	64
Markets, Stores, and Shopping Streets	66
Tokyo for Free	68
Festivals and Events	70

TOP 10 Moments in History

Senso-ji Temple in 1904

1 Founding of Senso-ji Temple

Discovered by two fishermen in their nets in 628, the golden image of the goddess Kannon was enshrined at the site of present-day Senso-ji. The temple has been rebuilt several times, and after air raids in 1945 a replica was put up in ferroconcrete.

2 Ota Dokan's Castle

The Musashino Plain was developed into a martial domain with the arrival of Ota Dokan, a minor feudal lord, in 1456. Dokan's fortress was built on a site named Edo, meaning "estuary mouth." A statue of the city founder stands at the Tokyo International Forum in Yurakucho.

3 Founding of Edo

The development of Edo village into Japan's de facto military capital began when future shogun Ieyasu Tokugawa arrived there in 1590. The land was reclaimed, water courses expanded, residences built, and Edo Castle developed into a huge citadel.

4 Long-Sleeves Fire

In 1657, priests at Hommyo-ji Temple in Hongo burned a "cursed" kimono owned by three girls who had died before becoming old enough to wear it. A gust of wind tore it away, starting fresh fires that claimed the lives of over 100,000 people.

5 47 Ronin Incident

In 1701, Lord Asano was ordered to commit ritual suicide for drawing his sword at court. His retainers, who had become *ronin*, or masterless samurai, avenged Asano's death by putting to death his opponent, Lord Kira, and placing his decapitated head on their master's grave. The act led the authorities to order the 47 loyal retainers to commit suicide.

6 Perry's "Black Ships"

On July 8, 1853, Commodore Matthew Calbraith Perry sailed four heavily armed ships into Edo Bay, to open Japan to diplomatic and trade relations. The "black ships" were a display of superior Western technology, a reminder of the astonishing progress that had bypassed the country.

Lithograph of Perry's "black ships"

7 Great Kanto Earthquake

At 11:58am on September 1, 1923, as people prepared lunch on charcoal braziers and gas burners, an earthquake measuring 7.9 on the Richter scale convulsed the city. Over 140,000 people were crushed or burned to death, and 45 per cent of the buildings were destroyed. This horrific event obliterated many traces of the past.

8 Tokyo Air Raids

US raids on Tokyo during World War II exacted a heavy toll on civilian lives. Tokyo suffered 102 raids in all, the worst on the night of March 9–10, 1945, when over 300 B-29 bombers, loaded with oil, jellied gasoline, and napalm, swooped over tightly packed residential areas to the east, killing between 80,000 and 100,000 civilians.

Pole vault, 1964 Tokyo Olympics

9 1964 and 2020 Olympics

The first games to be held in Asia and telecast live overseas, the summer Olympics of 1964 saw Tokyo reborn from the ashes of World War II, with modern stadiums, an expressway, and the start of the Shinkansen bullet train services. In 2020, just as the city was preparing to host the Olympic and Paralympic Games, the COVID-19 pandemic hit, forcing the events to be held in 2021 without spectators.

10 Assassination of Shinzo Abe

The assassination of Japan's longest-serving prime minister, Shinzo Abe, in 2022 shocked the country, which has one of the world's lowest rates of gun crime. He left behind a legacy of bold military reforms and economic policies, dubbed "Abenomics".

TOP 10 FAMOUS TOKYOITES

***Great Wave* by Katsushika Hokusai**

1 Katsushika Hokusai
A famous woodblock artist of the Edo period, Hokusai (1760–1849) published 30,000 sketches and 500 books.

2 Soseki Natsume
Regarded by many as Japan's greatest writer, Natsume (1867–1916) set several of his novels in Tokyo.

3 Ichiyo Higuchi
The face of the writer Higuchi (1872–96), who died from tuberculosis, graces the ¥5,000 Japanese note.

4 Junichiro Tanizaki
Tanizaki (1886–1965) explored themes of sexuality, Western modernity, and materialism in his novels.

5 Toshiko Yuasa
Japan's first female physicist, Yuasa (1909–80) was also the first woman in the country to work internationally as a scientist.

6 Akira Kurosawa
Kurosawa (1910–98), Japan's best-known film auteur, inspired Steven Spielberg and George Lucas.

7 Yoko Ono
Ono (b. 1933) was a reputed artist, musician, and experimental filmmaker long before she met John Lennon.

8 Hayao Miyazaki
Miyazaki (b. 1941) is the Oscar-winning director of *Spirited Away* and many other classics of Japanese animation.

9 Ryuichi Sakamoto
Sakamoto (b. 1952), a prolific composer, wrote the music for Bernardo Bertolucci's Oscar-winning film, *The Last Emperor.*

10 Marie Kondo
An author, TV host and a tidying expert, Marie Kondo (b. 1984) is a professional organizing consultant.

TOP 10 Historic Buildings

1 Hongan-ji Temple

MAP N5 ■ 3-15-1 Tsukiji, Chuo ■ 3541-1131 ■ www.tsukiji hongwanji.jp

Even in a city known for its architectural hybrids, this temple, inspired by Indian architecture, is extraordinary. Its designer, Chuta Ito, paid homage to the Indian origins of Buddhism in this 1935 building.

Imposing facade of Hongan-ji Temple

2 National Diet Building

MAP K4 ■ 1-7-1 Nagatacho, Chiyoda ■ 5521-7445 ■ Open 8am–5pm Mon–Fri ■ Closed public hols ■ www.sangiin.go.jp

Home to the Japanese Diet, or parliament, this building was completed in 1936. It has a pyramid-shaped dome and is divided into two main chambers – the Lower and Upper Houses. Weekday tours include the Public Gallery, Emperor's Room, and Central Hall.

3 Edo-Tokyo Open-Air Architectural Museum

Thirty historic buildings from around Tokyo dot this sprawling museum *(see p114)* located in Koganei Park. The buildings date from the late Edo period to the 1940s, and highlights include a farmhouse from the late 1800s and a 1920s bathhouse.

4 Kyu Iwasaki-tei Mansion

MAP F2 ■ 1-3-45 Ikenohata, Taito ■ 3823-8340 ■ Open 9am–5pm daily ■ Adm ■ www.tokyo-park.or.jp/park/format/index035.html

A fine example of Meiji-era syncreticism, this grand 1896 wooden residence was built by English architect Josiah Conder in a mix of Jacobean, Gothic, and Pennsylvanian country styles. Original features include coffered wood ceilings, stone fireplaces, parquet flooring, and Japan's first Western-style toilet.

5 Bank of Japan

The bank's *(see p75)* solid Neo-Classical outline was designed by Kingo Tatsuno, Japan's first Western-style architect. The 1896 building stands on the old site of the shogunate's former mint. A guided tour in English introduces the structure, its history, and present-day function.

Chamber of the National Diet Building

The main hall at Tokyo Station

6 Tokyo Station

Threatened with demolition on many occasions, the Tokyo Station building *(see p76)* has survived thanks to the efforts of preservation groups over the years. Designed by Kingo Tatsuno, the 1914 structure is faced with locally made bricks and reinforced with steel shipped from Britain and the United States.

7 Gokoku-ji Temple

MAP C1 ■ 5-40-1 Otsuka, Bunkyo ■ 3941-0764 ■ www.gokokuji.or.jp

The temple grounds have interesting features, including a belfry and a rare two-story pagoda. The main hall, with its colossal wooden pillars, massive copper roof, and dark interior full of priceless Buddhist artifacts, is the centerpiece of this grand complex.

8 Hattori Building

MAP M4 ■ 4-5-11 Ginza, Chuo ■ 3562-2111 ■ Open 10:30am–7pm daily ■ www.wako.co.jp

Commonly known as the Wako Building, this 1932 structure, created by Jin Watanabe, is a Ginza landmark. Named after the jeweler it houses, the building has appeared as a backdrop in several old movies. The interior is just as impressive as the exterior.

9 Ministry of Justice Building

MAP L4 ■ 1-1-1 Kasumigaseki, Chiyoda ■ 3580-4111

Although not open to the public, the building's exterior, well renovated in the 1990s, is worth a look. A German company, Ende and Böckmann, designed this 1895 redbrick structure in a style that mixes formal elegance with functionality.

10 Nikolai Cathedral

The 1891 cathedral *(see p43)* was lucky to survive the 1923 earthquake, with only its onion domes destroyed. A new green dome was placed on top of the cruciform Russian Orthodox church after the disaster, and impressive stained-glass windows were installed.

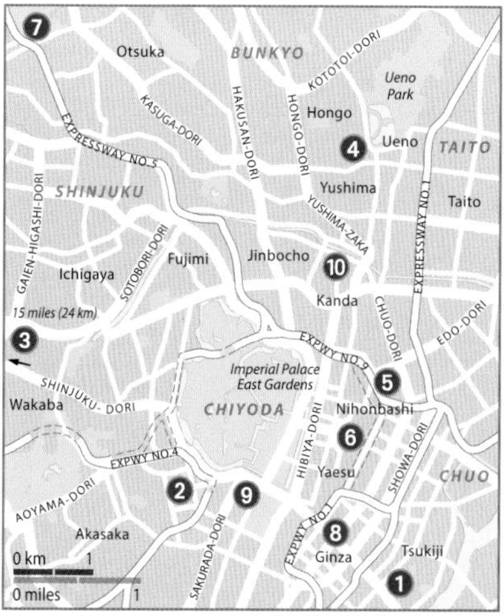

TOP 10 Places of Worship

1 Senso-ji Temple

This massive religious edifice *(see pp14–15)* is the focus of life in the Asakusa district. The sweeping roof of the main hall is visible from Kaminari-mon, one of the great gates to the temple. Inside the main hall, burning candles, incense sticks, and votive plaques add to the air of sanctity.

Richly decorated Senso-ji Temple

2 Sengaku-ji Temple

MAP C1 ■ 2-11-1 Takanawa, Minato ■ Open 7am–6pm daily (to 5pm Oct–Mar) ■ sengakuji.or.jp

The tombs of the 47 loyal *ronin* (retainers), who committed suicide after avenging their master's death *(see p38)*, can be found in this temple, which dates from 1612. The main hall was obliterated in the 1945 air raids but has been faithfully reconstructed.

3 Kanda Myojin Shrine

MAP F3 ■ 2-16-2 Sotokanda, Chiyoda ■ www.kandamyoujin.or.jp

Founded in 730, but first built on this site in 1616, this temple has been rebuilt many times. The current reconstruction of the 1616 design, has a copper roof, copper *torii* gate, and an ornate main entrance gate.

4 Nezu Shrine

MAP E1 ■ 1-28-9 Nezu, Bunkyo ■ 3822-0753

Established in 1706 by the fifth shogun, Tsunayoshi, Nezu Shrine is dedicated to Inari, the goddess of rice. The shrine grounds have retained most of the original structures. Tall cedars, ginkgo trees, and a carp pond create a strikingly natural setting. A painted gate, orange *torii* (gates), and bright banners add color.

5 Yushima Seido Temple

MAP F3 ■ 1-4-25 Yushima, Bunkyo ■ 3251-4606 ■ Open 9:30am–5pm daily (to 4pm Oct–Mar)

One of the few Confucian temples in Tokyo, Yushima Seido was founded in 1632. The current site and its great stone-flagged courtyard date from 1935. A statue of Confucius is located near the main gate.

6 Yasukuni Shrine

MAP D3 ■ 3-1-1 Kudankita, Chiyoda ■ 3261-8326 ■ Open 6am–6pm daily (to 5pm Nov–Feb) ■ www.yasukuni.or.jp

Politics and religion coexist uncomfortably at Yasukuni Shrine, dedicated to the souls of Japan's war

Entrance to Kanda Myojin Shrine

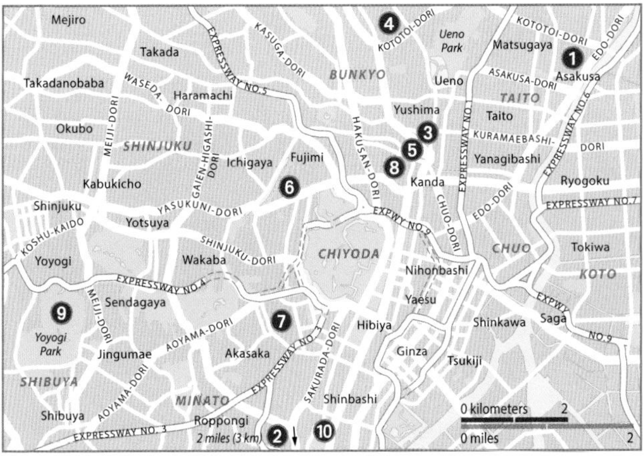

dead. Built in 1869, the shrine has some interesting features including an imposing *torii* gate, cherry trees, a pond-garden, and teahouse.

7 Hie Shrine

Reconstructed in 1958 after the Tokyo air raids, the 1659 building originally served as the protective shrine of Edo Castle. In gratitude, successive shoguns donated lavish gifts of swords and sacred horses to the shrine *(see p95)*. A line of orange *torii* gates forms a colorful tunnel through the grounds.

8 Nikolai Cathedral

MAP F3 ■ 4-1 Kanda-Surugadai, Chiyoda ■ 3295-6879 ■ Opening times vary, call ahead

Built with funds provided by a Russian czar and designed by English architect Josiah Conder, this late 19th-century Russian Orthodox church and its post-1923 earthquake additions are an interesting anomaly among the temples and shrines of the city. It was named after its founder St. Nikolai Kassatkin, a 19th-century missionary who converted thousands of Japanese in the northern island of Hokkaido.

9 Meiji Jingu Shrine

Dedicated to the souls of Emperor Meiji and his consort Empress Shoken, this impressive shrine *(see pp30–31)* was built in the pure Shinto architectural style. This is reflected in everything from its gravel forecourt, cypress pillars, and the clean lines of the main hall to the copper roof that floats majestically above it all.

Zojo-ji Temple, rebuilt in the 1970s

10 Zojo-ji Temple

The venue for the funerals of six Tokugawa shoguns, this temple *(see p97)* is best visited for its main gate, the San-mon, which dates from 1622, and Daibonsho, a 15-tonne bell. There's also a Himalayan cedar planted by former US president Ulysses S. Grant in 1879.

TOP 10 Museums

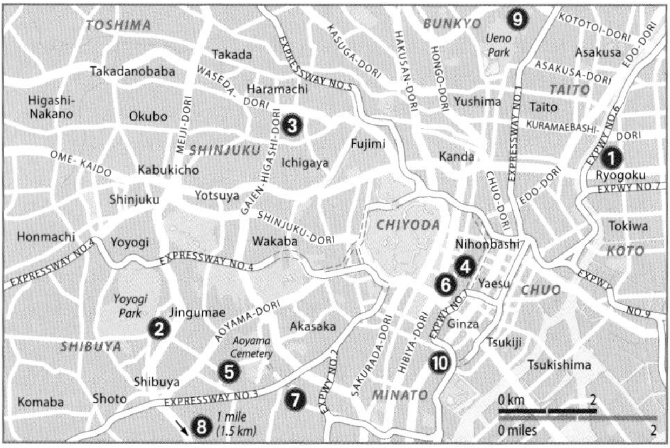

1 Edo-Tokyo Museum

MAP H3 ■ 1-4-1 Yokoami, Sumida ■ Closed for renovation until 2025 ■ www.edo-tokyomuseum.or.jp

This museum traces the history of Edo and Tokyo, charting its growth from a fishing village to a megacity. Exhibits cover both the creation of the city and the natural and human-made disasters that have reshaped it.

Ota Memorial Museum of Art

2 Ota Memorial Museum of Art

This fascinating museum's *(see p101)* extensive private collection of *ukiyo-e* woodblock prints is constantly displayed in new exhibitions. The images present a colorful cross-section of life in the city of Edo, from its streets and fish markets to the pleasure quarters.

3 Yayoi Kusama Museum

The first museum dedicated to Japan's favorite avant-garde artist, the Yayoi Kusama Museum *(see p107)* in Shinjuku is a must-visit for fans of contemporary art. The rooftop space is home to Kusama's iconic pumpkin sculptures. With only 200 visitors allowed a day, you'll need to get tickets in advance.

4 Intermediatheque

On the second and third floors of the Kitte shopping mall, resembling more of a high-design boutique than a traditional museum, Intermediatheque *(see p76)* displays eclectic items from the collection of the University of Tokyo. Cabinets of curiosities sit alongside contemporary installations and art. Adding to the quirkiness, gramophone record concerts are occasionally held for music lovers.

5 Nezu Museum

Housed in an elegant building designed by Kengo Kuma, this art museum *(see p100)* displays treasures from Japan and East Asia in changing exhibitions. Its ornamental gardens feature bronze sculptures and a contemporary-style teahouse.

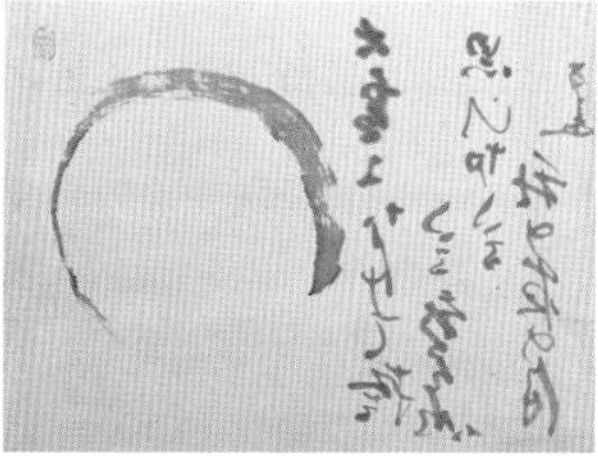

Exhibit at Idemitsu Museum of Arts

6 Idemitsu Museum of Arts

Housing one of the finest private collections of Japanese and Asian art in Tokyo, this museum *(see p82)* regularly rotates its exquisite Japanese, Chinese, and Korean ceramic ware and ancient pottery shards, calligraphy, and gold-painted screens. The collection includes over 15,000 items.

7 Mori Art Museum

MAP T5 ▪ 6-10-1 Roppongi, Minato ▪ 5777-8600 ▪ Open 10am–10pm Wed–Mon (to 5pm Tue) ▪ Adm ▪ www.mori.art.museum

There's no permanent collection here, but the enormous gallery spaces atop Roppongi Hills' Mori Tower regularly host some of Tokyo's biggest blockbuster art shows, with the likes of Takashi Murakami regularly showing.

Archeological relic, Tokyo National Museum

8 Tokyo Photographic Art Museum

MAP C1 ▪ Ebisu Garden Place, 1-13-3 Mita, Meguro ▪ 3280-0099 ▪ Open 10am–6pm Tue–Sun (to 8pm Thu & Fri) ▪ Adm (only for special shows) ▪ topmuseum.jp

The big names in Japanese and Western photography are shown at this premier photography and video art space. Five floors follow the history of photography, displaying 35,000 images and photo-related items. Special exhibitions, featuring some of the world's best photographic work, run through the year.

9 Tokyo National Museum

This huge museum offers the world's largest collection of Japanese art and antiquity. Permanent Japanese exhibits are displayed in the Honkan; archeological relics in the Heiseikan; Chinese, Korean, and Central Asian arts in the Toyokan; and Buddhist sculpture and scrolls in the Gallery of Horyu-ji Treasures *(see pp24–7)*.

10 Ad Museum Tokyo

The highly creative ad work on display at this fascinating venue *(see p83)* is sponsored by Dentsu, Japan's largest advertising operation. Permanent exhibits explore the long history of commercial art in Japan. A TV room makes it possible to view excellent commercials.

Creative exhibition at the Mori Art Museum in Tokyo

TOP 10 Art Galleries

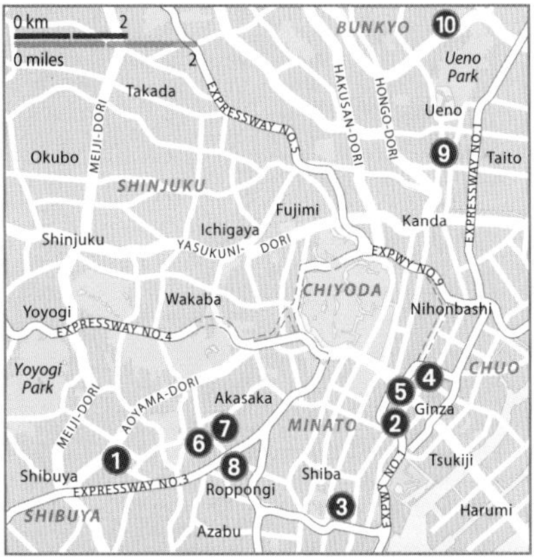

1 Spiral

MAP B6 ■ 5-6-23 Minamiaoyama, Minato ■ 3498-1171 ■ Open 11am–7pm daily ■ Adm ■ www.spiral.co.jp

Designed by leading architect Fumihiko Maki, this gallery presents art, music, film, and theater. A spiral ramp above a first-floor café leads visitors into the main gallery space.

2 Shiseido Gallery

MAP M5 ■ Tokyo Ginza Shiseido Bldg B1, 8-8-3 Ginza, Chuo ■ 3572-3901 ■ Open 11am–7pm Tue–Sat (to 6pm Sun) ■ gallery.shiseido.com/en

The chic Shiseido Gallery features contemporary Japanese and international artists, retrospectives, and fashion-linked exhibitions.

Striking Shiseido Gallery

3 The Tolman Collection

MAP E6 ■ 2-2-18 Shiba Daimon, Minato ■ 3434-1300 ■ Open 11am–7pm Wed–Sun ■ tolmantokyo.com

This gallery has around 1,500 contemporary Japanese prints, aquatints, etchings, lithographs, and woodblocks. Signed and numbered editions of work by artists such as Shingo Araki and Miki Gojo are also included.

4 Gallery Koyanagi

MAP N4 ■ 1-7-5 Ginza, Chuo ■ 3561-1896 ■ Open noon–6pm Tue–Sat ■ www.gallerykoyanagi.com

Leading Japanese and international photo and print artists showcase their works in this spacious commercial gallery tucked away on the eighth floor of an office building.

5 Ginza Graphic Gallery

MAP M5 ■ DNP Ginza Bldg, 1F, 7-7-2 Ginza, Chuo ■ 3571-5206 ■ Open 11am–7pm Mon–Sat ■ www.dnp.co.jp/gallery/ggg_e

Reopened in April 2016 following restoration, the Ginza Graphic Gallery is sponsored by DNP, one of Japan's largest printers. The gallery features works by Japanese graphic designers.

Dramatic glass building housing the National Art Center, Tokyo

6 National Art Center, Tokyo

Covering 516,668 sq ft (48,000 sq m), this massive space for art *(see p95)* comprises 12 exhibition rooms that host a variety of shows curated by NACT as well as by art associations from across Japan.

7 Suntory Museum of Art

MAP D5 ■ Tokyo Midtown Galleria, 3F, 9-7-4 Akasaka, Minato ■ Open 10am–6pm Wed–Mon (to 8pm Fri & Sat) ■ Adm ■ www.suntory.com/sma

Located in the Tokyo Midtown complex *(see p95)*, the SMA does not house a permanent collection. Instead, it hosts five or six themed exhibitions a year, with a focus on Japanese art, such as ceramics, glassware, and painting. On two Thursdays each month, the museum also organizes tea ceremonies in which *matcha* and traditional sweets are offered.

8 Taka Ishii Gallery

MAP T5 ■ 6-5-24 Roppongi, Minato ■ 3643-7010 ■ Open noon–6pm Tue–Sat ■ www.takaishiigallery.com/en

Specializing in solo as well as group exhibitions, Taka Ishii is a top spot for discovering up-and-coming Japanese artists. The gallery displays a wide variety of mediums, with exhibits including sculptures, paintings, light installations, and photography.

9 3331 Arts Chiyoda

MAP F2 ■ 6-11-14 Sotokanda, Chiyoda ■ 6803-2441 ■ Open 10am–9pm daily ■ www.3331.jp

A short stroll from the anime, manga, and computer-geek nexus of Akihabara, the exhibitions, interactive installations, and art workshops in this former school are guaranteed to be fun and eclectic.

Art workshop, 3331 Arts Chiyoda

10 SCAI – The Bathhouse

Located in a converted Edo-period bathhouse in the endearing old district of Yanaka, SCAI – The Bathhouse *(see p33)* is worth visiting for its building alone. Inside the minimalist high-ceilinged space, well-known experimental Japanese artists are showcased alongside emerging international artists. Old truly meets new here.

TOP 10 Modern and Contemporary Buildings

Mode Gakuen Cocoon Tower

1 Mode Gakuen Cocoon Tower

MAP U2 ■ 1-7-3 Nishishinjuku, Shinjuku

One of the slickest high rises to adorn Tokyo's cityscape, this 2008 building in Shinjuku was designed by Kenzo Tange Associates. Its criss-cross exterior pattern, rising up 50 floors, takes inspiration from a silkworm cocoon.

2 Fuji TV Building

This 1997 Odaiba landmark *(see p35)* was designed by Pritzker Architecture Prize winner Kenzo Tange, a key figure in the 1960s Metabolist movement. Tange connected Fuji TV Building's two towers with "streets in the skies" walkways, which he accented with a 1,350-tonne titanium sphere.

3 Asahi Beer Hall

MAP S3 ■ 1-23-1 Azumabashi, Sumida

Designed by Philippe Starck, Asahi Beer Hall is also known as Super Dry Hall and *Flamme d'Or*, after the giant golden sculpture on its roof. Next to it is another building, which resembles a pint of lager with a frothy top.

4 Tokyo Metropolitan Government Building

Stand back in the semicircular Citizen's Plaza, at the foot of the Tokyo Metropolitan Government Building *(see p109)*, to fully admire the symmetry of Kenzo Tange's 48-story, twin-towered creation. It cleverly channels Paris's Notre-Dame Cathedral via a very 20th-century Japanese prism.

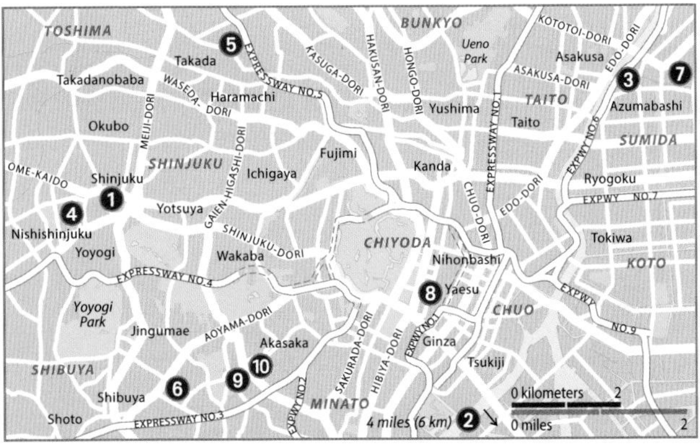

Stylish exterior of St. Mary's Cathedral

5 St. Mary's Cathedral

MAP C1 ■ 3-16-15 Sekiguchi, Bunkyo ■ 3941-3029

After the original Gothic Catholic cathedral here burned down during World War II, it was redesigned in 1964 by Kenzo Tange, who was also the architect responsible for the first Olympic Stadium at Yoyogi.

6 Prada Aoyama Building

Swiss architects Herzog & de Meuron made a splash in the fashionable Aoyama district in 2003 with this distinctive six-story contemporary boutique *(see p104)* for the famous Italian fashion house. Covered in rhomboid-shaped green-glass windows, the building looks like it has been bubble-wrapped.

7 Tokyo Skytree

Hard to ignore, Tokyo Skytree *(see p89)* is the world's tallest free-standing tower, visible from many parts of the city. For all its modernity, it is built along similar principles to those used by architects for centuries in order to protect temple pagodas against earthquakes.

Tokyo Skytree looming high above the city

8 Tokyo International Forum

Rafael Viñoly's 1996 construction *(see p82)* is symbolic of the end of 20th-century architecture in Tokyo. The construction is made up of several performance halls and a convention center hanging off an elliptical enclosure made of nearly 3,000 panels of tempered glass.

9 National Art Center, Tokyo

Kisho Kurokawa's final hurrah is this 2007 exhibition space *(see p95)* forming one point of the Roppongi Art Triangle. The undulating glass-and-steel facade is amazing, but even better is the soaring lobby dominated by two giant inverted cones.

10 21_21 Design Sight

MAP D5 ■ 9-7-6 Akasaka, Minato ■ 3475-2121 ■ www.2121designsight.jp

Like an iceberg, Tadao Ando's 21_21 Design Site is mainly underground with its presence announced only by the sharp-edge steel plate roofs of two low pavilions. The exhibition halls are made from polished concrete.

TOP 10 Gardens and Parks

from 1654. Standing near the garden entrance is a large black pine, planted in 1704, a miraculous survivor of earthquakes, fires, and air raids. The most interesting feature of this large garden is a tidal pond that brings in saltwater fish.

1 Canadian Embassy Garden

MAP C5 ■ Canadian Embassy 4F, 7-3-38 Akasaka, Minato ■ 5412-6200 ■ Open 9am–5:30pm Mon–Fri (book ahead)

Built across an upper terrace of the building, this stone garden was created by Masuno Shunmyo, one of the most innovative garden designers working in Japan today. Stones brought from Hiroshima form the Canadian Shield, and represent the relationship between Japan and Canada. ID is required for access.

2 Hamarikyu Garden

An original Edo-period garden, Hamarikyu *(see p82)* dates

Hamarikyu Garden, an urban retreat

3 Hibiya Park

Part of a feudal estate converted into a military parade ground, Hibiya Park *(see p81)* was Japan's first Western-style park when it opened in 1903. A lawn, rose garden, bandstand, and theater occupy the center of the park. A pond, with its original fountain in the shape of a heron, and a giant wisteria trellis lie in the western corner.

4 Mukojima Hyakka-en Garden

MAP D1 ■ 3-18-3 Higashimukojima, Sumida ■ 3611-8705 ■ Open 9am–5pm daily ■ Adm ■ www.tokyo-park.or.jp/teien/en/mukojima

This garden was completed in 1804 close to Sumida River *(see pp16–17)*, in what was once a district of temples and teahouses, and is the only surviving flower garden from the Edo Period.

5 Kiyosumi Garden

MAP H4 ■ 3-3-9 Kiyosumi, Koto ■ 3641-5892 ■ Open 9am–5pm daily ■ Adm ■ www.tokyo-park.or.jp/teien/en/kiyosumi

Rare rocks were shipped from all over the country in steam ships to create this garden, which was once part of an estate owned by the founder of Mitsubishi. A traditional teahouse overlooks a large pond and islets, where you can spot fish and turtles. Another eye-catching feature is an artificial hill, shaped into the likeness of Mount Fuji.

Koishikawa Koraku-en Garden

6 Koishikawa Koraku-en Garden

Tokyo's oldest garden *(see pp28–9)* re-creates famous scenes in miniature from Japan and China. A simple grass-covered knoll represents Mount Lu in China's Jiangxi Province, while a shallow stream stands in for Oikawa River in Kyoto.

7 Shinjuku Gyoen

Excelling at variety, this garden *(see p107)* was completed in 1772. The current garden, a multicultural masterpiece, is divided into French, English, and Japanese sections. An old, domed botanical greenhouse holds tropical plants.

8 Rikugi-en Garden

MAP C1 ■ 6-16-3 Honkomagome, Bunkyo ■ 3941-2222 ■ Open 9am–5pm daily ■ Adm ■ www.tokyo-park.or.jp/teien/en/rikugien

Completed in 1702, this garden was named after the six principles used in the composition of *Waka* poetry. While the garden's hidden symbolism is not easy to decipher, its curvaceous landscapes, simple Zen-style teahouses, and profusion of trees can be appreciated by all.

9 Yoyogi Park

MAP A5 ■ 2-1 Yoyogikamizonocho, Shibuya ■ 3469-6081 ■ Open 24 hours

A wide open area of grassy lawns and recreational facilities popular with families, cyclists, joggers, and skateboarders, Yoyogi Park makes a great spot for an impromptu picnic. Other attractions include a botanical garden, a bird sanctuary, and street performances every Sunday *(see p57)*.

10 Institute for Nature Study and Park

MAP C1 ■ 5-21-5 Shirokanedai, Minato ■ 3441-7176 ■ Open May–Aug: 9am–5pm Tue–Sun (Sep–Apr: 9am–4:30pm) ■ Adm ■ www.ins.kahaku.go.jp/english

A carefully preserved section of the Musashino Plain, the Institute for Nature Study's park is home to a variety of birds, insects, and turtles in addition to 8,000-plus trees. A small museum at the entrance traces Tokyo's declining greenery.

Spring blossom, Shinjuku Gyoen

TOP 10 Off the Beaten Path

Items for sale, Shimokitazawa

1 Shimokitazawa

MAP C1

On weekends, fashionable youth fill the narrow streets southwest of Shibuya for clothing, thrift stores, music clubs, and experimental theaters.

2 Ikebukuro

MAP C1

This northern district, set around a train station, offers mega department stores, Otome Road's manga and anime shops, and the Frank Lloyd Wright-designed school Myonichikan.

3 Daikanyama and Naka- Meguro

MAP C1

One stop southwest of Shibuya, Dainkanyama and Naka-Meguro are among the most pleasant areas of the city to browse trendy boutiques, convivial bars, and cafés. The cherry tree-lined Meguro River is also a prime spot during *hanami* season.

4 Kyu-Furukawa Gardens

MAP C1 ■ 1-27-39 Nishigahara, Kita ■ 3910-0394 ■ Open 9am–5pm ■ www.tokyo-park.or.jp/teien/en/kyu-furukawa

Rose beds and azalea bushes are a feature of Kyu-Furukawa Gardens. Admire them while sipping *matcha* (green tea) in the teahouse.

5 Toden Arakawa Line

The last of Tokyo's city-operated tram lines still operates between Waseda and Minowabashi, arcing 7.5 miles (12 km) across the north of the city. It's a retro treat that costs just ¥170 and offers an insight into the less touristy parts of Tokyo.

6 Kuramae

MAP G3

A short walk south of busy Asakusa, this neighborhood has been dubbed "Tokyo's Brooklyn" for good reason. Designers converge here, with the up-and-coming selling their wares in indie boutiques and craftspeople working away in artisanal studios. There are several hip cafés to stop by for good coffee and a rest after shopping.

Cherry tree-lined Meguro River

7 Ningyocho

MAP G4

Between Nihonbashi and the Sumida River is this *shitamachi* (old town Tokyo) district of temples, shrines, and traditional shops. Check out the craft stores along retail parade Amazake Yokocho.

8 Ryogoku

MAP G3 ■ National Sumo Stadium: 1-3-28 Yokoami, Sumida; 3623-5111 ■ Museum: open 10am–4:30pm Mon–Fri ■ www.sumo.or.jp

Tournaments lasting 15 days are held at this neighborhood's National Sumo Stadium in January, May, and September; at other times of the year, the building has a small sumo museum. Ryogoku also has several restaurants serving *chanko-nabe*, the hearty hotpot eaten by sumo wrestlers.

Sumo wrestlers prepare to compete

9 Japanese Sword Museum

MAP H3 ■ 1-12-9 Yokoami, Sumida ■ 6284-1000 ■ Open 9:30am–5pm Tue–Sun ■ Adm ■ www.touken.or.jp

Over 30 of the 120 Japanese swords here are designated National Treasures and are arguably the finest instruments of death ever made.

10 Kagurazaka

MAP D3 ■ 1-10 Akagi-Motomachi, Shinjuku ■ 3260-5071

Once a thriving geisha quarter, Kagurazaka's charming narrow cobbled streets, shops, and cafés evoke old-time Tokyo. The area's Akagi Shrine, however, received a contemporary makeover in 2010 by well-known architect Kengo Kuma.

TOP 10 SECRET SHOPPING SPOTS

Asagaya Pearl Center

1 Asagaya Pearl Center
MAP C1 ■ Suginami
A long shopping arcade known for selling sweets, kimonos, and crafts.

2 Jimbocho
MAP E3 ■ Chiyoda
Home to winter sports stores and bookshops of rare and used books.

3 Kappabashi-dori
MAP Q2 ■ Taito
A street with over 100 stores selling kitchenware *(see p89)*.

4 Ochanomizu
MAP F3 ■ Chiyoda
Shops here specialize in musical instruments and vintage guitars.

5 Kichijoji Sunroad
Musashino
An arcade with a retro vibe selling everything from daily essentials to vintage kimonos.

6 Shimo-Kitazawa
MAP C1 ■ Setagaya
A hip neighborhood known for vintage clothing and used record stores.

7 Nippori Fabric Town
MAP F1 ■ Arakawa
Along Chuo-dori, there are 90 stores selling textiles and sewing accessories.

8 Sunamachi Ginza
MAP R3 ■ Koto
An old-fashioned shopping street lined with food stalls and family-run shops.

9 Sugamo Jizo-dori
MAP C1 ■ Toshima
Known as "Harajuku for Grandmas", this street has stores selling snacks, clothing for seniors, and lucky red underwear.

10 Togoshi Ginza
MAP C2 ■ Shinagawa
Tokyo's longest *shotengai* (shopping street) has thrift stores and snack stalls.

TOP 10 Children's Attractions

1 Joypolis

Located in the Decks Tokyo Beach mall in Odaiba *(see p34)*, this amusement center has ride simulators, arcade games, and virtual reality attractions. Little kids will enjoy looking for treasure while playing Pirate's Plunder. For the older kids and adults, a virtual Wild River ride and zombie laser tag game await.

Visitors at Joypolis

2 Drum Museum

MAP Q3 ■ 2-1-1 Nishiasakusa, Taito ■ 3842-5622 ■ Open 10am–5pm Wed–Sun ■ Adm

This interactive museum has a collection of over 800 *taiko* (drums) from all over the world. The highlight are the Japanese festival drums. Skins with a blue sticker can be played, but with care, while those with a red mark cannot be touched. A stickerless drum can be played freely.

3 Kite Museum

Displayed at this delightful museum *(see p77)* are around 400 kites, shaped variously as squid, sumo wrestlers, and Mount Fuji. Some are illustrated with the faces of manga characters, samurai warriors, and Kabuki actors.

4 KidZania

MAP G6 ■ Lalaport Toyosu, 2-4-9 Toyosu, Koto ■ 0570-064012 ■ Open 9am–3pm, 4–9pm ■ Adm ■ www.kidzania.jp

Children under 12 can experience the working world of adults by role-playing in dozens of jobs, such as TV anchor, pizza chef, barber, banker and cop in a realistic city setting. They even get paid in "kidZos", the official currency of KidZania.

5 Railway Museum, Omiya

For kids, or adults, who like trains, this museum *(see p113)*, located north of Tokyo, makes for a great day out. There are more than 30 trains on display here, ranging from steam engines to early *shinkansen* (bullet train). The highlight for many will be the various simulators, where you can try driving a train yourself.

6 Ghibli Museum

Hayao Miyazaki's animations, surreal landscapes, whimsical characters, and fanciful sets can be seen here *(see p116)*. Kid's will love the "wonderland" atmosphere.

The vibrant exterior of Ghibli Museum

7 National Museum of Nature and Science

The model of a giant whale greets visitors to this museum *(see p87)*, which has dinosaur displays, exhibits on botany, fossils, asteroids, and oceanography, among other attractions.

8 Tokyo Disney Resort®

Mickey and pals will pull out all the stops for kids (and adults) in this fantasyland *(see p116)* of castles, magic mountains, haunted mansions, Polynesian villages, and steamboat rides.

9 Tokyo Dome City

MAP E2 ■ 1-3-61 Koraku, Bunkyo ■ 5800-9999 ■ Open 9:30am–9pm ■ Adm ■ www.tokyo-dome.co.jp

This amusement park has a free-fall parachute ride, Sky Flower, but the highlight is the rollercoaster Thunder Dolphin. LaQua, the park's other section, features a selection of restaurants, shops, and spas.

Ferris wheel, Tokyo Dome City

10 National Museum of Emerging Science and Innovation

Known more simply as Miraikan, this fascinating museum *(see p35)* in Odaiba is packed with hands-on attractions to entertain and educate both adults and kids. The exhibits have excellent English translations. The museum's "Create Your Future" zone allows visitors to interact with androids (human-like robots).

TOP 10 SHOPS FOR KIDS

Kiddy Land, set over five floors

1 Kiddy Land
MAP S4 ■ 6-1-9 Jingumae, Shibuya ■ www.kiddyland.co.jp/harajuku
Store filled with cuddly character models and games.

2 Tomica
MAP N3 ■ Tokyo Station, 1-9-1 Marunouchi, Chiyoda ■ www.takaratomy.co.jp
Shop specializing in Takara Tomy goods.

3 Hakuhinkan Toy Park
MAP M5 ■ 8-8-11 Ginza, Chuo ■ www.hakuhinkan.co.jp
Specialty store selling toys and games.

4 BorneLund
MAP S4 ■ 1-3-12 Jingumae, Shibuya ■ 5411-8022
Good-quality imported toys.

5 Yamashiroya Toy Shop
MAP F2 ■ 6-14-6 Ueno, Taito ■ 3831-2320
A six-floor shop stuffed with toys.

6 Animate
MAP B1 ■ 1-20-7 Higashiikebukuro, Toshima ■ www.animate.co.jp
Nine floors of anime and manga items.

7 Hello Kitty Store
MAP H2 ■ Tokyo Skytree Solamachi, 1-1-2 Oshiage, Sumida ■ 5610-2926
Sells Hello Kitty merchandise, and tickets to Sanrio Puroland.

8 Kotobukiya
MAP G2 ■ 1-8-8 Sotokanda, Chiyoda ■ en.kotobukiya.co.jp
Home to goods related to Nintendo, Star Wars, Marvel, and more.

9 Pokémon Center Mega Tokyo
The best merchandise of the "Pocket Monsters" anime series *(see p56)*.

10 Kuramae–Asakusabashi Toy Street
MAP G3 ■ Kuramae, Taito
Wholesalers showcase their wares along this traditional toy street.

Top 10 Pop Culture Venues

Performers at the Hello Kitty 40th anniversary parade in Sanrio Puroland

1 Sanrio Puroland

MAP B2 ■ 1-31 Ochiai, Tama ■ Opening times vary, check website ■ Adm ■ en.puroland.jp

Dedicated to Japan's most famous feline, Hello Kitty, this theme park has attractions for kids, song and dance shows, and opportunities to meet Kitty and other Sanrio characters.

2 Takeshita-dori

MAP B5 ■ Takeshita-dori, Shibuya

Packed with boutiques, subculture junk, cutesy accessories, kitsch, and fetish costumery, this loud, abrasive but fun street is frequented by Japan's alternative youth.

3 Design Festa Gallery

MAP R4 ■ 3-20-18 Jingumae, Shibuya ■ 3479-1442 ■ Open 11am–8pm daily ■ www.designfesta.com/en

The biannual Design Festa event encourages freedom of expression. This gallery, run by the organizers of the event, is open for temporary exhibitions all year round.

4 Pokémon Center Mega Tokyo

MAP C1 ■ Sunshine City 2F, 3-1-2 Higashiikebukuro, Toshima ■ 5927-9290 ■ Open 10am–8pm ■ www.pokemon.co.jp

This is the biggest of several stores in Tokyo selling Pokémon-related merchandise. Expect to find no end of themed clothes, figures, toys, and snacks as well as Pokémon statues.

5 Tokyo Anime Center

MAP B6 ■ 1-21-3 Jinnan, Shibuya ■ 6416-3977 ■ Open 11am–8pm Tue–Sun ■ www.animecenter.jp

Formerly located in bustling Akihabara, the center caters to die-hard anime fans and features temporary as well as permanent exhibitions showcasing anime-production techniques.

6 Tokyo Big Sight

MAP D2 ■ Tokyo International Exhibition Center, 3-11-1 Ariake, Koto ■ 5530-1111 ■ www.bigsight.jp

This busy venue hosts expos and other major events through the year. During the biannual, two-day Design Festa *(see p70)*, Tokyo Big Sight sees over 50,000 visitors.

The striking Tokyo Big Sight building

7 Ghibli Museum

Make sure you book ahead to visit this popular and charming museum *(see p116)*, which brings to life the characters and fantasy environments of the animated movies created by Hayao Miyazaki and his colleagues at Studio Ghibli.

8 Sunday in the Park

Tokyo's theater of dress spills over from busy Harajuku into Yoyogi Park *(see p51)* every Sunday, where you may chance upon costumes reflecting every trend since the 1950s. Live bands set up during the afternoon along the sidewalk between the park and Olympic pavilions.

9 Center Gai

MAP B6 ■ 12-3 Udagawacho, Shibuya

A lively pedestrian street crammed with inexpensive bars, cafés, and restaurants as well as stores selling music records, cell phones, clothes, and jewelry. Center Gai is the epicenter of Japanese youth culture – full of teens and early twentysomethings.

Shoppers thronging Center Gai

10 Nakano Broadway

MAP C1 ■ 5-52-15 Nakano, Nakano ■ Open noon–8pm daily (some stores may vary)

A smaller and less frantic version of Tokyo's *otaku* mecca, Akihabara, Nakano Broadway is anime and manga heaven. The complex is a short walk from Nakano Station, packed with stores selling everything from comics to game consoles to collectible figurines.

TOP 10 CULTURAL PHENOMENA

Hello Kitty attraction

1 Hello Kitty
Launched in 1974, this helplessly naive but adorable creature has a button nose and, inexplicably, no mouth.

2 Cosplay
Cosu-pure, or costume play, refers to dressing in outfits worn mainly by manga or anime characters.

3 Capsule Hotels
Architect Kisho Kurokawa's recently demolished Nakagin Capsule Building inspired the idea of the capsule hotel.

4 Maid Cafés
Young women in white tights, pink hair, lace caps, and aprons respectfully serve tea and cakes.

5 Purikura
These photo booths provide instant digital photos that can be enhanced with all manner of designs to create manga-style selfies.

6 Manga Kissa
For a cup of coffee at a *kissa*, short for *kissaten* (café), manga fans can access hundreds of comic books.

7 Hip Fashion "Tribes"
Harajuku and Shibuya are full of cyber-punks and "Gothic Lolita" – locals in black makeup and Victorian frills.

8 Otaku
Otaku – geeks or nerds – are passionate about anime, manga, video games, and cute female star merchandise.

9 Love Hotels
There are over 20,000 short-stay love hotels in Tokyo alone, which feature various fantasy themes.

10 Pachinko
Pachinko, or Japanese pinball, is considered lowbrow, but there are parlors on many shopping streets.

TOP 10 Entertainment Venues

Performance of *The Rose of Versailles* at Takarazuka Theater

1 Takarazuka Theater

MAP M4 ■ 1-1-3 Yurakucho, Chiyoda ■ www.kageki.hankyu.co.jp

Established in 1914, the Takarazuka stages sentimental plays featuring an all-female cast, unlike Kabuki, which is an all-male preserve. *The Rose of Versailles*, with its rich costumes and dashing heroes, is a favorite. Synopses are provided in English.

2 National Theater

MAP D4 ■ 4-1 Hayabusacho, Chiyoda ■ 3265-7411 ■ www.ntj.jac.go.jp/en

The two stages at this performing arts complex regularly stage a variety of traditional entertainment, including Kabuki, Bunraku (puppetry), court music, and dance. English language earphone guides are available.

3 New National Theater

MAP A4 ■ 1-1-1 Honmachi, Shibuya ■ 5351-3011 ■ www.nntt.jac.go.jp/english

The three stages – Play House, Opera Palace, and the Pit – cater to different audiences. Interpretations of Western classics by Japanese directors are excellent, though most visitors prefer visual events like modern dance.

4 Bunkamura Theater Cocoon

MAP A6 ■ 2-24-1 Dogenzaka, Shibuya ■ 3477-9111 ■ www.bunkamura.co.jp/english

Housed in the huge Bunkamura culture and arts center, the Cocoon hosts concerts, musicals, and opera. A medium-sized theater, it is best known for performances of contemporary dance, ballet, and its long involvement with flamenco dance and music troupes from Spain.

5 National Noh Theater

MAP B4 ■ 4-18-1 Sendagaya, Shibuya ■ 3423-1331 ■ www.ntj.jac.go.jp/en

The traditional performing art of Noh, based on ancient tales of avenging spirits and wandering ghosts, is more like contemporary dance than a play. Read the English leaflet provided to make sense of the plot.

Musicians at a concert in Suntory Hall

6 Suntory Hall

MAP D5 ■ 1-13-1 Akasaka, Minato ■ 3505-1001 ■ www.suntory.com/culture-sports/suntoryhall

Suntory Hall is said to have the best acoustics in Tokyo. This classical music concert hall sees top local and international performers gracing its stage. Once a month, it holds a free pipe organ recital during lunchtime.

7 Asakusa Engei Hall

MAP R2 ■ 1-43-12 Asakusa, Taito ■ 3841-6545

Traditional comic storytelling takes place here. The seated narrators perform alone, with the barest of props, usually just a fan. Although it is exceedingly difficult for foreigners to follow, it is worth a visit for the atmosphere at least.

A show at Kabuki-za Theater

8 Kabuki-za Theater

Reconstructed in 2013, this Baroque Japanese revivalist-style building *(see p81)* stages Kabuki shows. Full dramas of three to four acts can extend throughout an afternoon or evening. Single-act tickets provide a shorter, more accessible entrée into Kabuki for the first timer.

9 Shinbashi Enbujo

MAP N5 ■ 6-18-2 Ginza, Chuo ■ 3541-2600

This theater stages period dramas, whose plots are strong on the conflict between love and duty. "Super Kabuki," a modern dramatic form devised by veteran actor Ennosuke Ichikawa, guarantees to keep even non-Japanese audience members alert.

10 Tokyo Dome

MAP E2 ■ 1-3-61 Koraku, Bunkyo ■ www.tokyo-dome.co.jp

Known locally by its nickname as the "Big Egg," this central Tokyo stadium is the home of top baseball team Yomiuri Giants; attending a game during the season is great fun. The venue is also used for pop concerts.

TOP 10 MOVIES SET IN TOKYO

1 Stray Dog (1949)
A rare chance to see what Tokyo's downtown streets looked like in the post-war era.

2 Tokyo Story (1953)
Yasujiro Ozu's classic, set mostly in a working-class area of the city, explores the collapse of the Japanese family.

3 Godzilla (1954)
Awakened by the A-bomb, the giant lizard stumbles through the city until pacified by Japanese scientists.

4 Diary of a Shinjuku Thief (1968)
Nagisa Oshima's film explores the minds of young Japanese radicals in this audacious film.

5 Shall We Dance? (1996)
Tokyo night scenes form the backdrop to this story of a salaryman who finds a higher purpose in ballroom dancing.

6 Lost in Translation (2003)
Sofia Coppola's comedy-drama captures the cultural confusion of two Americans in Tokyo.

7 Babel (2006)
Oscar-nominated Rinko Kikuchi plays the mute Chieko in the Tokyo strand of this globetrotting movie.

8 Tokyo Sonata (2008)
How a middle-class Tokyo family reacts when the father loses his job and tries to keep it a secret.

9 Tokyo Tribe (2014)
Yakuza gang violence, martial arts action, and hip-hop music all collide in this fast-paced fantasy set in a divided Tokyo of the future.

10 Shoplifters (2018)
A Palme d'Or winner, this movie takes a harrowing look at a Tokyo family that survives through petty crime.

Scene from *Tokyo Tribe*

TOP 10 Onsen and Sento

1 Toshimaen Niwa no Yu

MAP C1 ■ 3-25-1 Koyama, Nerima ■ Open 10am–11pm daily ■ Adm ■ www.seibu-leisure.co.jp/niwanoyu

Located in a traditional garden, next to the Toshimaen amusement park, this spa has multiple zones, including indoor and outdoor mineral-rich hot springs, Jacuzzis, and a Finnish-style sauna. There's even a bar if you fancy a cocktail between soaks.

2 Komparu-yu

MAP M5 ■ 8-7-5 Ginza, Chuo ■ 3571-5469 ■ Open 2–10pm Mon–Fri (to 8pm Sat) ■ Adm

In business since 1863, this *sento* (public bathhouse) is about as retro as they come. The tiled bath walls here have beautiful murals, some depicting carp, flowers, and Mount Fuji. Komparu-yu has two large bathtubs, and depending on the season, irises, citrons, lavender, or other fragrant flowers are sprinkled into the tub.

3 Tomei Onsen Sakura

MAP C1 ■ 5-4-24 Komagome, Toshima ■ Open 10am–11pm daily ■ Adm ■ www.sakura-2005.com/english

Situated in the quiet environs of Komagome, this bathhouse has separate hot spring baths (indoors and outdoors) for men and women. There is also an on-site restaurant, hot-stone sauna, beauty salon, and a relaxation lounge, so there's plenty to do between dips. Note that there's a no tattoo policy.

4 Take no Yu

MAP D6 ■ 1-15-12 Minamiazabu, Minato ■ 3453-1446 ■ Open 3:30–11:30pm Tue–Thu, Sat & Sun ■ Adm

Established in 1913, and given a much-needed makeover in the early 2000s, this natural hot spring bathhouse is known for its almost black water, a result of volcanic ash and peat. Take no Yu is located close to Roppongi, making it one of Tokyo's most easily accessible *onsen*.

5 Hakone

One of the most popular side trips out of Tokyo is to Hakone *(see p114)*, known for the hot spring facilities that dot its hills and valleys, and the shores of Lake Ashi. The town has many traditional *ryokan* (inns), which are great for a night of pampering. They all have baths, sometimes communal and sometimes – at a steeper cost – en suite.

The volcanic valley of Owakudani in Hakone

6 Shimizu-yu

MAP C6 ▪ 3-12-3 Minamiaoyama, Minato ▪ 3401-4404 ▪ Open noon–midnight Mon–Thu, noon–11pm Sat & Sun ▪ Adm

In one of Tokyo's most fashionable areas, just a few streets away from Omotesando's luxury shops, lies this simple *sento*. It has concentrated carbonate-spring and silk baths, offering a pampering experience. Amenities including soap, shampoo and fresh towels are provided here.

7 Spa LaQua

MAP E1 ▪ Tokyo Dome City, 1-1-1 Kasuga, Bunkyo ▪ Open 11am–9am daily ▪ Adm ▪ www.laqua.jp

This fancy spa complex, next to Tokyo Dome, is home to indoor and outdoor baths, saunas, restaurants, and more. LaQua is geared towards adults – no under-5s are allowed at any time, and under-17s are allowed only until 6pm.

8 Kamata Onsen

MAP B2 ▪ 2-23-2 Kamatahoncho, Ota ▪ 3732-1126 ▪ Open 10am–12:30am daily ▪ Adm

There's nothing fancy about this old-fashioned *sento*, but it offers a clean and peaceful environment where you can unwind. It has a variety of baths filled with *kuro-yu* (black water) drawn from Tokyo Bay's sea bed.

9 Maenohara Onsen

MAP C1 ▪ 3-41-1 Maenocho, Itabashi ▪ Open 9am–midnight daily ▪ Adm ▪ www.sayanoyu dokoro.co.jp/english

A little out of the way in Itabashi (about 30 mins from Shinjuku), Maenohara Onsen has 14 baths that are fed by natural hot-spring water. Surrounded by lovely foliage, the outdoor baths here are particularly soothing and offer respite from the city's bustle.

10 Kawaguchi-ko

Lake Kawaguchi *(see p114)* is a popular overnight trip from Tokyo. Stay in one of the *ryokan* around the lake to enjoy stunning views of Mount Fuji while relaxing in a bath.

TOP 10 BATHING TIPS AND ETIQUETTE

A *sento* with communal showers

1 Know the Difference
An *onsen's* baths are fed by natural hot-spring water, while a *sento's* are not.

2 Amenities
Most *onsen* provide towels, soap and shampoo to their customers. However, in a *sento*, you often need to bring your own.

3 Get Naked
In almost all bathhouses, even some with mixed-gender bathing areas, you must get completely naked.

4 Feeling Shy?
You can use your small wash towel to cover up a little, but it can't go in the bath water.

5 Wash First
The golden rule of any bathhouse – wash and rinse well before entering the baths.

6 Don't Splash
Baths are for soaking. Splashing, swimming, and talking loudly are not permitted.

7 Watch the Heat
Many baths are piping hot. Take regular breaks and make use of the bathhouse's water cooler.

8 Skip the Sake
No drinking or eating is allowed in the baths, nor is bathing while under the influence of alcohol.

9 The Tattoo Rule
Some bathhouses don't allow bathers with tattoos, an outdated rule to deter *yakuza* (mafia) members.

10 No Photos
Visitors are not allowed to take photos or videos in the bathhouse.

Top 10 Restaurants

Low tables with *tatami* mats, Asakusa Imahan

1 Asakusa Imahan

An early exponent of beef dishes, Asakusa Imahan opened its first restaurant *(see p91)* in 1895. One of the specialties here is *shabu-shabu*, wafer-thin slices of prime beef cooked at your table in a pot of boiling water and served with seasonal vegetables. Seating is at low tables on *tatami* mats.

2 Bird Land

This Michelin-starred grill *(see p85)* is known for its high-quality *yakitori*, sticks of charcoal-broiled chicken doused in a slightly sweet soy-based sauce. Diners who are fond of *yakitori* will enjoy the chicken cuts here, which are closer to the lighter Chinese kebabs than the Turkish or Central Asian varieties. The restaurant offers good sake and wine lists.

The sophisticated interior of Bird Land

3 Kappo Yoshiba

Housed in a former sumo training stable, with a sumo ring, Kappo Yoshiba *(see p91)* serves *chanko-nabe*, a robust stew of vegetables, chicken, and fish. This healthy, but calorific, dish is the staple diet of sumo wrestlers.

4 Kanda Yabu Soba

In an old wooden building, this venerable restaurant *(see p79)* serves classic Edo-period, hand-made *soba* (buckwheat noodles) along with vegetable and pickle side dishes. Given its popularity, it fills up quickly at lunch time and on weekends, so prior booking is recommended.

5 Den

Chef Zaiyu Hasegawa's restaurant *(see p105)* is a regular fixture on international "best" lists thanks to Hasegawa's creative, contemporary Japanese cuisine. The menu is simple and features just the *omakase* (chef's choice), so you will never have the same dining experience here twice.

6 Maru

This sleek restaurant *(see p85)* has a long counter table facing onto an open kitchen. It's a stylish place to sample the *kaiseki* style of fine dining at an affordable price. The lunchtime menu is particularly good value.

7 Kyubey

This restaurant *(see p85)* in Ginza serves sushi at its most sublime, and it won't be a surprise to hear that Kyubey has several branches located in luxury hotels. Such high-end, exquisitely prepared sushi is a costly affair, but the lunch courses are a more affordable option.

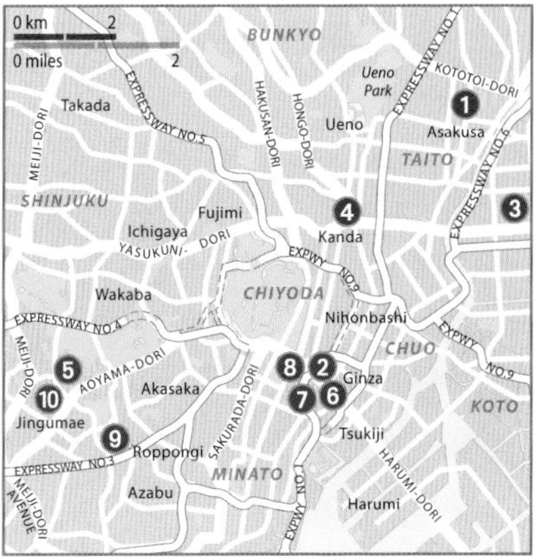

8 RyuGin

Although it's been relocated from Roppongi to the sleek Tokyo Midtown Hibiya complex, RyuGin *(see p85)* still serves the most innovative *kaiseki* in the city. Owner-chef Seiji Yamamoto's attention to detail has earned the restaurant a three-star Michelin rating. The exquisitely arranged dishes vary every day, depending on what's in season.

9 Gonpachi

If you've watched the film *Kill Bill*, this *izakaya (see p99)* might look familiar – the famous The Bride vs Gogo fight scene was shot here. While the restaurant is known for its delectable, top-notch *sumiyaki* (char-grilled skewers of meat, seafood, and vegetables), the menu also features tempura, *soba* noodles, and other dishes that go well with sake.

10 Maisen

The popular Maisen chain *(see p105)* is famous for its delicious *tonkatsu* (*deep*-fried pork cutlets with their own brand of dipping sauce), served with rice, a bed of shredded cabbage, and miso soup. Seafood alternatives include delicately fried shrimp and oysters served with a dribble of lemon. The Aoyama branch of Maisen, located in an old converted bathhouse, is perhaps the most atmospheric branch to dine in.

Customers dining at the busy Maisen branch in Aoyama

TOP 10 Cafés and Bars

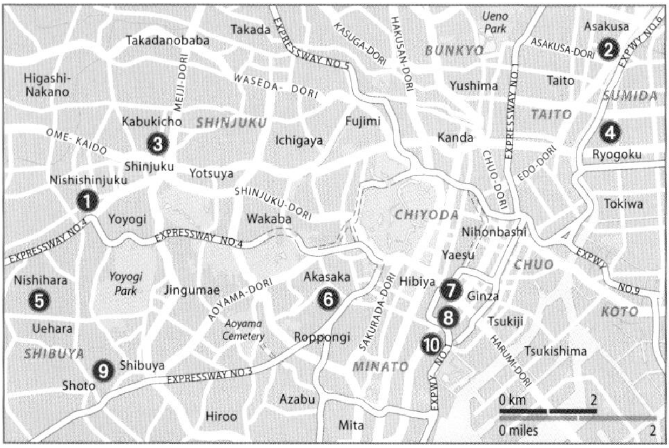

1 New York Bar

MAP T3 ■ 3-7-1-2 Nishishinjuku, Shinjuku ■ 5323-3458 ■ Open 5–11pm Sun–Wed (to midnight Thu–Sat) ■ restaurants. tokyo.park.hyatt.co.jp

Housed in the Park Hyatt hotel, this sophisticated bar featured prominently in the movie *Lost in Translation*. There's a cover charge after 6:30pm and live jazz music performed nightly by top artists.

New York Bar in the Park Hyatt hotel

2 Kamiya Bar

MAP R3 ■ 1-1-1 Asakusa, Taito ■ 3841-5400 ■ Open 11:30am–10pm Wed–Mon

The oldest Western-style bar in town, this Tokyo institution was established in 1880. The bar was set up by Kamiya Denbei, who also built Japan's first brandy distillery. Once favored by writers and artists, the bar still serves its signature *denki-bran*, a cocktail made with cognac, gin, and wine.

3 Golden Gai

This bustling quarter *(see p107)*, filled with scores of tiny bars housed in two-story wooden buildings, has hung on in Shinjuku since just after World War II. Most bars have a theme and not all are welcoming to tourists, but it's still well worth a visit.

4 Popeye

MAP G3 ■ 2-18-7 Ryogoku, Sumida ■ 3633-2120 ■ Open 11am–2:30pm & 3–11:30pm daily

Conveniently located within walking distance from the famous Sumo Stadium, this convivial bar does its best to cater to Tokyo's unquenchable thirst with some 70 craft beers on tap, including the city's best selection of Japanese beers.

5 Sasagin

MAP A5 ■ 1-32-15 Uehara, Shibuya ■ 5454-3715 ■ Open 5–9pm Mon–Sat

This is a great place to sample different types of Japanese sake.

Tastes range from the syrupy sweet to the highly rated acerbically dry. Top-grade sake, such as the divine *dai-ginjo*, is served chilled.

6 Pink Cow

Popular with the expat crowd, this American-owned, lively bar *(see p98)* and gallery space serves up an excellent selection of cocktails. Be aware, however, that the house specialty is CBD-infused drinks. It is not a bad place for dinner either, with reasonably priced Californian and Mexican fare. There are events, including stand-up comedy and live music, most nights.

7 Cha Ginza

MAP M4 ■ 5-5-6 Ginza, Chuo ■ 3571-1211 ■ Open 11am–6pm Tue–Sat

A shortened version of the Japanese tea ceremony here includes whisking the creamy brew into a bubbly froth and serving it with a Japanese sweet. The second floor serves *sencha* (ordinary green leaf tea).

8 Café de l'Ambre

MAP M5 ■ 8-10-15 Ginza, Chuo ■ 3571-1551 ■ Open noon–8pm Mon–Sat (to 7pm Sun)

One of Tokyo's longest-running coffee shops, this place has been in business since 1948. Make your choice from the 30-odd blends including quite a few aged varieties. The retro ambience of the place is priceless and makes for an unforgettable visit.

Beer taps at Goodbeer Faucets

9 Goodbeer Faucets

MAP A6 ■ Crossroad Bldg 2F, 1-29-1 Shoto, Shibuya ■ 3770-5544 ■ Open 4pm–midnight Mon–Fri, noon–midnight Sat, noon–11pm Sun ■ shibuya.goodbeerfaucets.jp

The craft beer scene in Japan has blossomed in recent years. This centrally located spot is a superb place offering more than 40 craft beers on tap in a stylish, sophisticated setting. The food here is also a cut above the usual pub fare.

10 TwentyEight

MAP M6 ■ Conrad Tokyo, 1-9-1 Higashishinbashi, Minato ■ 6388-8745 ■ Open 8am–10pm daily

Set on the 28th floor of the Conrad Tokyo hotel, this stylish bar offers stellar cocktails, superb snacks, and gentle jazz piano music. With its subdued lighting and floor-to-ceiling windows, TwentyEight offers spectacular views over Tokyo Bay and is one of the most romantic spots in town.

A barista at work, Café de L'Ambre

Top 10 Markets, Stores, and Shopping Streets

Grand Mitsukoshi in Nihonbashi

1 Mitsukoshi

This is the head branch *(see p18)* of Japan's oldest department store business, founded in 1673 by Takatoshi Mitsui, a kimono fabric merchant. The store is so beloved, that the Mitsukoshimae Station was named after it. Aside from the many items on sale, it's worth visiting for its grand interior decorations, including a giant statue of the Goddess of Sincerity. The store is a stickler for tradition, with hundreds of uniformed staff bowing respectfully to customers as they open the store each day.

2 Toyosu Fish Market

MAP H6 ■ 6-6-1 Toyosu, Koto ■ www.toyosu-market.or.jp/enl

The Tokyo Metropolitan Central Wholesale Produce Market, better known as Tsukiji Fish Market, moved to these state-of-the-art premises, across Tokyo Bay in Toyosu. This is the site of the famous tuna auctions that take place early in the morning.

3 Tsukiji Outer Market

The fish market *(see p82)* may have moved but there are still hundreds of vendors in the Tsukiji Outer Market, which has styled itself as the premier place to go food shopping in central Tokyo. There's plenty to see and taste here among the intricate streets, so pick up a map from the Information Center (Plat Tsukiji).

4 Naka-dori

MAP F4 ■ 1-chome to 3-chome Marunouchi, Chiyoda

This tree-lined, flagstoned street is Maranouchi's main commercial spine, along which you'll find many international and local fashion boutiques as well as contemporary sculptures. The trees are illuminated with thousands of LED bulbs every winter.

5 Takeshita-dori

It's great for people watching and trend-spotting, but avoid this narrow Harajuku shopping street *(see p102)* if you're not keen on crowds. The stores here have their fingers firmly on the pulse of teen fashions, hence it's usually busy.

6 Ginza Six

MAP M6 ■ 6-10-1 Ginza, Chuo ■ Shops: open 10:30am–8:30pm daily; restaurants: open 11am–11pm daily ■ www.ginza6.tokyo

Spread over six floors, this luxury complex in Ginza houses high-end fashion brands, including flagship stores of Vivienne Westwood, Saint Laurent, Jimmy Choo, and Fendi. It also has contemporary art installations, restaurants, deli stores, and even a Noh theater.

Plush interiors of Ginza Six

7 Ameyoko Market

MAP F2 ■ 4-chome ■ Ueno Station

Initially a post-war black market specializing in sweets made from potato, Ameyoko has developed into an amazing street with over 500 stalls and small stores built under the JR railway tracks. A favorite spot for very fresh food goods, especially fish.

8 Yanaka Ginza

This shopping street *(see p32)* may be quite small, but it's lined with some 70 independent businesses. Yanaka Ginza is characterized by the post-war period and offers a rare slice of traditional shopping. Look out for sculptures of cats on the buildings, a nod to the many strays that pad around the area.

Wickerwork for sale, Yanaka Ginza

9 mAAch ecute

MAP F3 ■ 1-25-4 Kandasudacho, Chiyoda ■ Open 11am–8pm daily ■ www.ecute.jp/maach

The decommissioned Manseibashi Station and the arches under the train tracks have been transformed into this stylish shopping and dining complex. Browse chic home goods and artisan foods from across Japan.

10 Coredo Muromachi

This stylish retail complex *(see p18)*, split over three buildings, is home to a host of fashion and interior design boutiques, traditional delis, sweet shops, bars, and restaurants. Zone in on Coredo Muromachi 3 for contemporary Japanese home and fashion design, as well as gourmet foods.

TOP 10 ARTS STORES

Itoya, a stationery emporium

1 Itoya
MAP N5 ■ 2-7-15 Ginza, Chuo ■ 3561-8311 ■ www.ito-ya.co.jp
Nine floors with all kinds of stationery.

2 Bingo-ya
MAP C1 ■ 10–6 Wakamatsucho, Shinjuku ■ www.bingoya.tokyo
A selection of local folk arts and crafts.

3 Tokyu Hands
MAP R5 ■ 12-18 Udagawacho, Shibuya ■ www.tokyu-hands.co.jp/en
DIY, crafts, hardware, and home items.

4 Takumi
MAP M5 ■ 8-4-2 Ginza, Chuo ■ 3571-2017 ■ Closed Fri
Folk crafts, ceramics, and toys.

5 Japan Traditional Crafts Aoyama Square
MAP C5 ■ 8-1-22 Akasaka, Minato ■ kougeihin.jp
Traditional Japanese crafts.

6 Blue & White
MAP J6 ■ 2-9-2 Azabu-Juban, Minato ■ www.blueandwhitejapan.com
Items in indigo-dyed blue and white.

7 Hara Shobo
MAP E3 ■ 2-3-3 Kandajinbocho, Chiyoda ■ www.harashobo.com
Ukiyo-e woodblock prints and illustrated books.

8 Sagemonoya
MAP C3 ■ Palais Eternal Bldg, 704, 4-28-20 Yotsuya, Shinjuku ■ www.netsuke.com
Sells hanging purses and pipe cases as well as carved wood sculptures.

9 Oriental Bazaar
MAP S4 ■ 5-9-13 Jingumae, Shibuya ■ orientalbazaar.co.jp
Gifts and souvenirs on Omotesando.

10 2k540 Aki-Oka Artisan
MAP C3 ■ 5-9 Ueno, Taito ■ www.jrtk.jp/2k540
A lively market selling traditional and contemporary crafts.

TOP 10 Tokyo for Free

1 Shrines and Temples

Religious sites rarely charge admission and the city has thousands of free temples and shrines. Most architecturally interesting are Senso-ji Temple *(see pp14–15)* and Meiji Jingu Shrine *(pp30–31)*.

Contrasting architecture in Tokyo

2 Architecture

Few cities are as adventurous in their architectural style as Tokyo, making it a pleasure to admire buildings old and new. Contrast the grand dames, such as Tokyo Station *(see p41)*, with more modern constructions, such as the Prada Aoyama Building *(see p49)*.

3 Public Art

Roppongi Hills *(see p94)* and Tokyo Midtown *(see p95)* are scattered with interesting pieces of sculpture and public art. In Shinjuku *(see pp106–9)*, check out the artworks surrounding Shinjuku I-Land.

4 Museums

Museum of Yebisu Beer: MAP C2; 4-20-1 Ebisu, Shibuya; 5423-7255; 11am–7pm Tue–Sun; www.sapporobeer.jp/english/brewery/y_museum ▪ Meguro Parasitological Museum: MAP C2; 4-1-1 Shimomeguro, Meguro; 3716-1264; 10am–5pm Wed–Sun; www.kiseichu.org

The entry is free (tasting charges vary) for the Museum of Yebisu Beer – which tells the story of the famous Japanese beer – or the quirky Meguro Parasitological Museum – where you'll find jars filled with such stomach-churning exhibits as the world's longest tapeworm.

5 Viewing Observatories

For a great city view, the free 45th-floor observation deck at the Tokyo Metropolitan Government Building *(see p48)* is hard to beat. The glittering vistas from the upper floors of the Shibuya Hikarie *(see p103)* are equally seductive.

6 Yoyogi Park

The chief location for the 1964 Summer Olympics, Yoyogi Park *(see p51)* has become one of Tokyo's most

Relaxing in Yoyogi Park

beloved open spaces. It's very lively on Sundays, when bands perform and rockabilly dancers mingle with a rainbow array of fashion tribes around the entrance near Meiji Jingu Shrine.

7 Origami Kaikan

MAP F2 ■ 1-7-14 Yushima, Bunkyo ■ 3811-4025 ■ Open 9:30am–4:30pm Mon–Sat ■ www.origamikaikan.co.jp

Learn about the gentle art of paper folding at Origami Kaikan, a building that includes free exhibitions as well as a workshop, where you can watch artisans creating paper art.

Aerial view of Shibuya Crossing

8 Shibuya Crossing

The statue and mural of Hachiko, Tokyo's most famous canine, gets lost amid the crowds flowing around Shibuya Station. The crossing (also known as Shibuya Scramble) here *(see p103)*, enveloped by giant LCD screens and neon lights, is one of Tokyo's most iconic sights.

9 Walking Tours

The city offers 13 different free guided tours starting from the Tokyo Metropolitan Government Building *(see p109)*. Itineraries include a tea ceremony and a trip out to a nature park in the suburbs. For details visit www.gotokyo.org/en/guide-services.

10 Ginza's Galleries

Ginza is all about high-end, fashionable shopping, but it costs nothing to enjoy the free shows at the area's many commercial art galleries.

TOP 10 BUDGET TIPS

The Imperial Palace East Gardens

1 Garden Hop
Tokyo's gardens *(see p50)* rarely cost more than ¥200 to enter, and the Imperial Palace East Gardens *(see p12)* is free.

2 Bargain Accommodation
Opt for chain business hotels, such as Toyoko Inn *(www.toyoko-inn.com)* or members of the Japanese Inn Group *(www.japaneseinngroup.com)*.

3 Public Transportation
Use the prepaid Suica or Pasmo cards to ride trains, subways, and buses around Tokyo.

4 Eat Lunch
Set lunches at many restaurants are a bargain at around ¥1000 or less.

5 Flea Markets
Pick up bargain souvenirs from flea markets at Nogi Shrine *(see p95)* and Yasukuni Shrine *(see p42)*.

6 Happy Hours
Many bars offer happy hours between 5 and 7pm.

7 Discount Card
The Grutto Pass *(www.rekibun.or.jp/grutto)* provides free or discounted admission to over 100 museums and attractions.

8 Save on Souvenirs
Look for ¥100-stores like the Daiso chain, where the likes of chopsticks and snacks are all priced at ¥100.

9 Wi-Fi
Download the Japan Wi-Fi Auto-Connect app *(www.ntt-bp.net/jw-auto/en/index.html)* to access free Wi-Fi across Tokyo.

10 Do Your Research
Check Tokyo Cheapo *(www.tokyocheapo.com)* for more ideas on how to make your yen go further.

TOP 10 Festivals and Events

Festivities on New Year's Day

1 New Year's Day

Jan 1

Millions of Japanese welcome the New Year with visits to Shinto shrines and Buddhist temples throughout Tokyo in early January. The most popular venues are Meiji Shrine *(see pp30–31)* and Senso-ji temple *(see pp14–15)*, where bells are rung to celebrate the New Year.

2 Coming-of-Age Day

MAP B5 ▪ 1-1 Kamizonocho, Yoyogi, Shibuya ▪ 3379-5511 ▪ 2nd Mon in Jan

The age of consent in Japan is 20, which is a milestone celebrated in Tokyo by ceremonies at major shrines. Meiji Shrine *(see pp30–31)*, where an archery display is held to mark the event, is one of the most popular venues.

3 Water Purification Rites

MAP F3 ▪ Kanda Myojin Shrine ▪ Mid-Jan

Cleansing rituals are held at several shrines throughout Tokyo in winter. The *kanchu-misogi* sees men and women stand in pools full of blocks of ice and douse themselves with freezing buckets of water.

4 Tokyo Marathon

MAP A4 ▪ Feb

The Japanese take pride in their marathon runners, particularly women, who have won gold medals in past Olympics. Competing is a serious business, with very strict entrance rules and requirements. The run begins at the Tokyo Metropolitan Government Building.

5 Horseback Archery

MAP S2 ▪ Sumida Park, Taito-ku ▪ Mid-Apr

Yabusame, or horseback archery, was integral to the samurai arts of war. During this event, men in samurai gear charge their mounts through Sumida Park, aiming to strike three targets in rapid succession.

6 Design Festa

May/Nov

This biannual event, Asia's largest art festival, features 7,000 Japanese as well as international artists, musicians, and performers from every conceivable genre. Drawing over 50,000 visitors, this festival also presents fashion shows and *cosplay* exhibitionists. The 2-day event is held at Tokyo Big Sight *(see p56)*.

Design Festa display

7 Sanja Festival

MAP R2 ▪ Senso-ji Temple, 2-3-1 Asakusa, Taito ▪ www.senso-ji.jp ▪ 3rd weekend of May

Tokyo's largest festival honors two brothers who found a statue of Kannon, the Goddess of Mercy, in their fishing nets *(see p15)*. The spirits of the brothers and the shrine's deities are carried in portable shrines through the streets.

8 Kanda Matsuri

MAP F3 ■ Kanda Myojin Shrine, Sotokanda, Chiyoda ■ www.kandamyoujin.or.jp ■ Mid-May

One of Tokyo's three major festivals, the Kanda Matsuri is held in odd-numbered years. It features music and dance, but the highlight is the Heian-period costume parade, a procession of floats and *mikoshi* (portable shrines).

Kanda Matsuri parade

9 Sumida River Fireworks

Last Sat in July

Around 1 million Tokyoites converge on the riverbanks near Asakusa to see over 20,000 fireworks light up the skies and the Sumida River. The best views are from Komagata Bridge or between Shirahige and Kototoi bridges *(see pp16–17)*.

10 Seven-Five-Three Festival

Nov 15

Children who have reached the ages of three, five, or seven are dressed up in pint-sized traditional kimonos and taken to shrines to pray for their well-being at this delightful event. The numbers signify ages once considered milestones when child mortality was high. The occasion is also a great photo opportunity.

Children dressed for Seven-Five-Three Festival

TOP 10 FLOWER AND PLANT EVENTS

Plum flowers in full bloom

1 Plum Blossom Viewing
MAP F2 ■ Late Jan–early Mar
The blossoms at Yushima Tenjin Shrine attract Tokyoites.

2 Cherry Blossom Viewing
Late Mar–mid-Apr
Crowds picnic under the pink blossoms in parks and gardens.

3 Azalea Festival
MAP E1, L2 & M2 ■ Apr 10–May 15 ■ Adm
Azaleas bloom at Nezu Shrine and the Imperial Palace East Gardens.

4 Peony Displays
MAP F2 ■ Mid-Apr
Pink, red, and yellow peonies can be viewed at Ueno Park's Tosho-gu shrine.

5 Iris Viewing
MAP B5 & D1 ■ Early–mid-Jun
Visit the stunning iris gardens at Meiji Shrine and Horikiri.

6 Morning Glory Fair
MAP C1 ■ Jul 6–8
Vendors sell potted morning glories in the grounds of Kishimojin Temple.

7 Chinese Lantern Plant Fair
MAP R1 ■ www.senso-ji.jp ■ Jul 9–10
Popular fair held in Senso-ji temple.

8 Lotus Blossoms
MAP F2 ■ Mid-Jul–Aug
An array of pink lotuses bloom in Shinobazu Pond in Ueno Park.

9 Chrysanthemum Festival
MAP B4 & C4 ■ Late Oct–mid-Nov
Shinjuku Gyoen garden has an exhibition of chrysanthemums.

10 Fall Leaves
Late Nov
Red maples, russet fall leaves, and yellow ginkgoes bloom in the parks and old Edo-period gardens.

Tokyo
Area by Area

The Shinjuku skyline, emblazoned with neon signs

Central Tokyo 74

Ginza 80

Ueno, Asakusa, and Oshiage 86

Roppongi and Akasaka 94

Aoyama, Harajuku, and Shibuya 100

Shinjuku 106

Farther Afield 112

TOP 10 Central Tokyo

The historic city and the site of Edo Castle, with its moats, stone ramparts, and bridges, once defined the imperial power structure: the merchant classes to the east, and samurai and lords to the south and west. In some ways, the power structure has remained visibly intact, with the Imperial Palace (on the site of the former Edo Castle) at the center; National Diet (parliament), law courts, and police headquarters to the south; and the financial center to the east. The area has been transformed by a series of fires, earthquakes, air raids, and developers, yet the outlines of the core city remain intact. Modern-day central Tokyo has also developed as a lively tourist attraction with excellent sightseeing and shopping options around every corner.

Lamppost on the decorative Nihonbashi Bridge

CENTRAL TOKYO

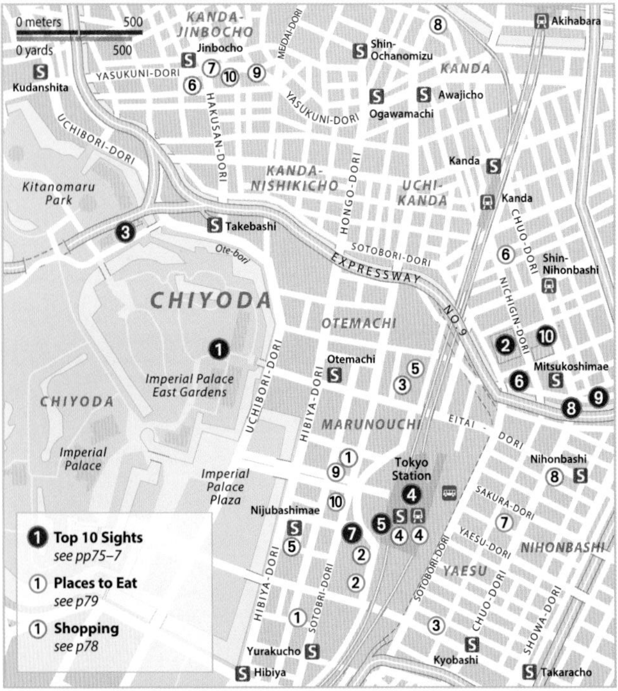

Imperial Palace East Gardens, with a view of the tea pavilion

1 Imperial Palace Grounds

The sprawling Imperial Palace Grounds *(see pp12–13)* offer a respite from the frenetic city life, and are home to some of Tokyo's most iconic sights, such as the Nijubashi Bridge. The Imperial Palace East Gardens alone are worth the walk here, especially the pond area with its waterfall, stone lantern, bridge, tea pavilion, and pebbled beach. The garden is resplendent with plum blossoms, spring cherry, and azaleas in spring; irises and lilies in summer; and bush clover, camellias, and maple leaves in the fall.

2 Bank of Japan

MAP N2 ■ 2-1-1 Nihonbashihongokucho, Chuo ■ 3279-1111 ■ English-language tour: 3:15–4:15pm every other Tue ■ www.boj.or.jp/en/index.htm

The bank was aptly built on the site of the shogun's former gold mint. Kingo Tatsuno, who designed Tokyo Station, was responsible for this earlier 1896 building. The Bank of Japan is divided into two sections – the New Building where financial transactions occur and the Old Building, which has a few offices, is more of an architectural exhibit. The building represents the first Western-style building designed by a Japanese architect.

3 National Museum of Modern Art (MOMAT)

MAP L1 ■ 3-1 Kitanomarukoen, Chiyoda ■ 5777-8600 ■ Open 10am–5pm Tue–Thu, Sat & Sun (to 8pm Fri & Sat) ■ Adm ■ www.momat.go.jp/english

Visitors can take a look at the exhibitions that draw on this museum's excellent collection of over 9,000 works from leading Japanese artists, past and present, plus some important European pieces. The range of art on display here is impressive, including gilded screens, woodblock prints, and striking video works.

National Museum of Modern Art

The elegant red-brick Tokyo Station

4 Tokyo Station

MAP N3 ■ 1 Marunouchi, Chiyoda

Designed by Kingo Tatsuno, this 1914 red-brick building recently underwent a major restoration that brought back its twin cupolas. Rendered in Queen Anne style, it is said to be modeled on Station Amsterdam Centraal. The south side of the building is occupied by a hotel and the north by the small but interesting Tokyo Station Gallery, hosting regularly changing exhibitions.

BUILDING EDO CASTLE

After its expansions were completed in 1640, Edo Castle was the largest citadel in the world, with 30 bridges, 28 armories, 21 watchtowers, and 110 gates. Gigantic slabs of stone were shipped from Izu Peninsula to make impregnable walls. More than 100 men were hired to drag the stones from the ship. The stones have survived; the wooden castle has not.

5 Marunouchi

MAP M2

Between the old facade of Tokyo Station and the peaceful outer grounds of the Imperial Palace *(pp12–13)*, the high-rise Marunouchi business district is a reminder that Tokyo is a fast-paced, ultra-modern city. The area is home to offices, slick malls like Kitte and Oazo *(see p78)*, museums, boutiques, and excellent restaurants and cafés. From late autumn until mid-February, the streets of Marunouchi are decorated with fairy lights and illuminated sculptures, making it feel like one of the most festive parts of the capital.

6 Currency Museum

Operated by the Bank of Japan, this museum has a dizzying variety of currencies from the past and present on display, along with money-related items from around the world.

7 Intermediatheque

MAP M3 ■ 2-7-2 Marunouchi, Chiyoda ■ 5777-8600 ■ Open 11am–6pm Tue–Thu & Sun (to 8pm Fri & Sat) ■ www.intermediatheque.jp/en

This is one of Tokyo's most eclectic and interesting museums, displaying key pieces from the collection of the University of Tokyo – from dinosaur skeletons to contemporary art.

8 Nihonbashi Bridge

MAP P2 ■ Nihonbashi, Chuo

Occupying a special place in Tokyo's history, Nihonbashi Bridge *(see p18)* is shown in many *ukiyo-e* woodblock prints. The current structure dates from 1911, and is decorated with statues of symbolically powerful animals, including lions and dragons. In the run-up to the 1964 Tokyo Olympics, waterways were filled in and a complex system of overhead expressways built. Distances throughout Japan are still measured from the bronze pole here, called the Zero Kilometer marker.

Nihonbashi Bridge

Colorful kites at the Kite Museum

9 Kite Museum

MAP G4 ■ 1-8-3 Nihonbashi-muromachi, Chuo ■ 3275-2704 ■ Open 11am–5pm Mon–Sat ■ Adm ■ www.taimeiken.co.jp/museum.html

This tiny museum above a restaurant displays 400 kites, mostly collected by the restaurant's original owner, from around Japan and China. The Japanese kites are adorned with real and mythological figures, as well as animals and natural landscapes. Kite frames are made from bamboo, and the sails from *washi*, a strong paper made from a type of mulberry tree. Picture outlines are painted in black India ink to restrict the flow of pigments.

10 Mitsui Memorial Museum

Treasures of Japanese and Asian art collected down the generations by the Mitsui family are displayed in this elegant museum *(see p18)*, housed in the grand, early 20th-century Mitsui Main Building. Among the delightful and valuable items displayed – of which there are more than 4,000 – is a reconstruction of the interior of the celebrated Joan tea-ceremony room in Inuyama. Other highlights include calligraphy works, Noh drama masks, and swords.

THE OLD AND NEW OF CENTRAL TOKYO

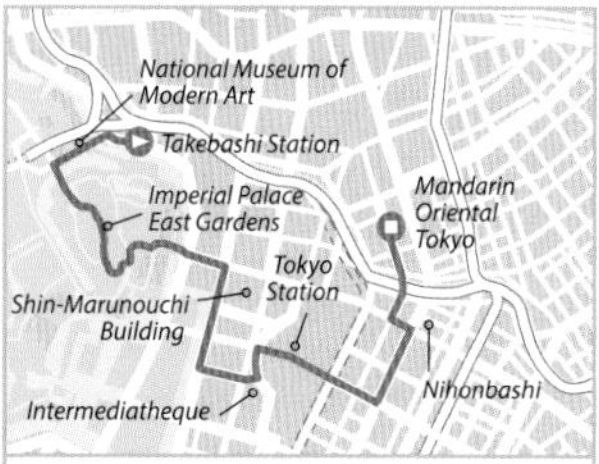

MORNING

Arrive at Takebashi Station around 10am, after the commuter crowds have dispersed, and head (via exit 1b) for the **National Museum of Modern Art** *(see p75)*, which houses Japanese and Western-style paintings, prints, sculptures, and photography from the 20th century onwards. Afterwards, stroll around the picturesque **Imperial Palace East Gardens** *(see p75)*, the site of Edo Castle, the shogun's citadel. Here, you can climb the ruins of a keep for a view of the gardens. Then, head to the nearby skyscrapers of the **Marunouchi** business district, for a satisfying lunch at one of the many cafés and restaurants in the towering **Shin-Marunouchi Building** *(see p78)*.

AFTERNOON

After lunch, stop by the eclectic **Intermediatheque** museum, which has exhibits on everything from natural history to Buddhist art, and then walk through Tokyo Station, a superb 1914 structure that also has sprawling, modern underground malls. From there, continue north to the **Nihonbashi** district *(see pp18–19)* to explore some of the oldest continuously operating businesses in the world, including traditional stores such as *washi* paper merchant Haibara and ultra-modern complexes such as the Coredo Muromachi, which has three buildings focusing on fashion, interior design, sweet shops, bars, and restaurants. Finish with a drink at the stylish Mandarin Bar in the sumptuous **Mandarin Oriental Tokyo** hotel *(see p128)*.

See map on p74

Shopping

1 Shin-Marunouchi Building

MAP M3 ■ 1-5-1 Marunouchi, Chiyoda ■ www.marunouchi.com/building/shinmaru

This shopping mall has more than 150 stores and restaurants, ranging from boutiques and jewelers to bakeries.

Interior of the Kitte shopping mall

2 Kitte

MAP M3 ■ 2-7-2 Marunouchi, Chiyoda ■ marunouchi.jp-kitte.jp

The former Central Post Office building is now a shopping mall. It offers an excellent selection of local retailers specializing in fashion, household goods, and traditional crafts with a contemporary flair.

3 Oazo

MAP N2 ■ 1-6-4 Marunouchi, Chiyoda ■ www.marunouchi.com/building/oazo

This dazzling glass complex of stores, restaurants, and cafés also has a massive English bookstore, Maruzen.

4 Tokyo Character Street

MAP N3 ■ B1 First Avenue Tokyo Station, 1-9-1 Marunouchi, Chiyoda ■ 3210-0077

Lovers of Japanese pop culture should zone in on this collection of stores devoted to beloved comic book and TV characters, including Rilakumma, Pokemon, and Ultraman.

5 Nakadori

MAP M2 ■ Marunouchi 2, Chiyoda

Marunouchi's central street, Nakadori is home to skyscrapers like Shin-Maru, luxury boutiques, and cafés. The street looks gorgeous during winter when it is lit up.

6 Hara Shobo

MAP E3 ■ 2-3 Kandajinbocho, Chiyoda ■ www.harashobo.com

This specialist offers a huge variety of woodblock prints. These range from affordable prints that cost around ¥10,000 to pieces that are worthy of being exhibited at museums.

7 Ebisu-do Gallery

MAP E3 ■ Inagaki Bldg 4F, 1-9 Kandajinbocho, Chiyoda ■ 3219-7651

This gallery specializes in *ukiyo-e* woodblock prints. Originals start at ¥15,000, but you can pick up a good reproduction for only around ¥3,000.

8 Yamamoto Yama

MAP P3 ■ 2-5-1 Nihonbashi, Chuo ■ 3271-3273

In addition to serving fine Japanese teas and confections, tea-ceremony instruments, such as bamboo whisks, iron water pots, and ceramic tea bowls, can be purchased here.

9 Ohya Shobo

MAP E3 ■ 1-1 Kandajinbocho, Chiyoda ■ www.ohya-shobo.com

Established in 1882, this store sells *ukiyo-e* woodblock prints and antique books at reasonable prices.

10 Isseido

MAP E3 ■ 1-7 Kandajinbocho, Chiyoda ■ www.isseido-books.co.jp

Dating from 1913, this antiquarian bookstore retains its original Art Deco features. The second floor has old English books and rare maps.

Places to Eat

PRICE CATEGORIES
Price ranges are for dinner for one, with a drink. Lunchtime menus are usually less expensive.

¥ under ¥3,000 ¥¥ ¥3,000–¥8,000
¥¥¥ over ¥8,000

1 Brasserie aux Amis
MAP M3 ■ Shin-Tokyo Bldg, 1F, 3-3-1 Marunouchi, Chiyoda ■ 6212-1566 ■ ¥¥
Dine on rustic brasserie food in a charming setting and wash down your *plat du jour poisson* with a drink from the long wine list.

2 Bar de España Muy
MAP M3 ■ Tokyo Bldg Tokia, 2F, 2-7-3 Marunouchi, Chiyoda ■ 5224-6161 ■ ¥¥
Relax at this fun tapas bar serving Catalan-style food. Try the black squid with a glass of cava.

3 Dhaba India
MAP N3 ■ Sagami Bldg, 1F, 2-7-9 Yaesu, Chuo ■ 3272-7160 ■ ¥¥
This Southern Indian restaurant offers thali sets and masala dosas served with basmati rice.

Masala dosa at Dhaba India

4 Tokyo Ramen Street
MAP N3 ■ B1 First Avenue Tokyo Station, 1-9-1 Marunouchi, Chiyoda ■ ¥
Eight ramen restaurants run stalls serving variations of the noodle dish.

5 Washoku En
MAP N2 ■ Oazo Bldg, 5F, 1-6-4 Marunouchi, Chiyoda ■ 5223-9896 ■ Closed Sun ■ ¥¥
Feast on a fine selection of regional Japanese cuisine and simple dishes, such as grilled salmon belly and smoky eggplant.

6 DevilCraft Kanda
MAP F3 ■ 4-2-3 Nihonbashi-muromachi, Chuo ■ Closed Mon & Tue ■ www.en.devilcraft.jp ■ ¥¥
Enjoy Chicago-style pizza paired with DevilCraft's own craft brews, which range from fruity wheat beers to heady imperial IPAs.

7 Yukari
MAP N3 ■ 3-2-14 Nihonbashi, Chuo ■ 3271-3436 ■ Closed Sun ■ ¥¥¥
Known for its fish dishes made with delicious relishes and seasoning. Try the conger eel, snapper, and crab with Japanese citrus or opt for the chef's *kaiseki* course.

8 Kanda Yabu Soba
MAP F3 ■ 2-10 Kandaawajicho, Chiyoda ■ 3251-0287 ■ Closed Wed ■ ¥
As the restaurant's name suggests, the specialty here is handmade soba. Enjoy yours hot or cold.

9 Wattle
MAP M3 ■ Shin-Marunouchi Bldg, 6F, 1-5-1 Marunouchi, Chiyoda ■ 5288-7828 ■ ¥¥
Crisp Australian wines are perfect complements for the Aussie fusion dishes that are served here.

10 Breeze of Tokyo
MAP M3 ■ Marunouchi Bldg, 36F, 2-4-1 Marunouchi, Chiyoda ■ www.breezeoftokyo.com ■ ¥¥¥
Superb French cuisine is served in a chic setting with great views over the city. There's an extensive cocktail and wine list and 30 types of champagne.

See map on p74

TOP 10 Ginza

Plate at the Idemitsu Museum of Arts

The site of the shogun's original silver mint, Ginza has always been synonymous with commerce and wealth. After a disastrous fire in 1872, the government commissioned the Irish architect Thomas Waters to rebuild the district in brick. The new quarter established Ginza as a leader in commerce, leisure, and fashion. It was the site of Japan's first gas lamps, trolley cars, and Western-style department stores. The epicenter of Ginza is the 4-chome district, a crossing dominated by modern stores. Though a premier cosmopolitan shopping and cultural experience, with its teahouses, incense and calligraphy stores, high-end sushi restaurants, and the very traditional Kabuki-za Theater, it is also firmly Japanese.

GINZA

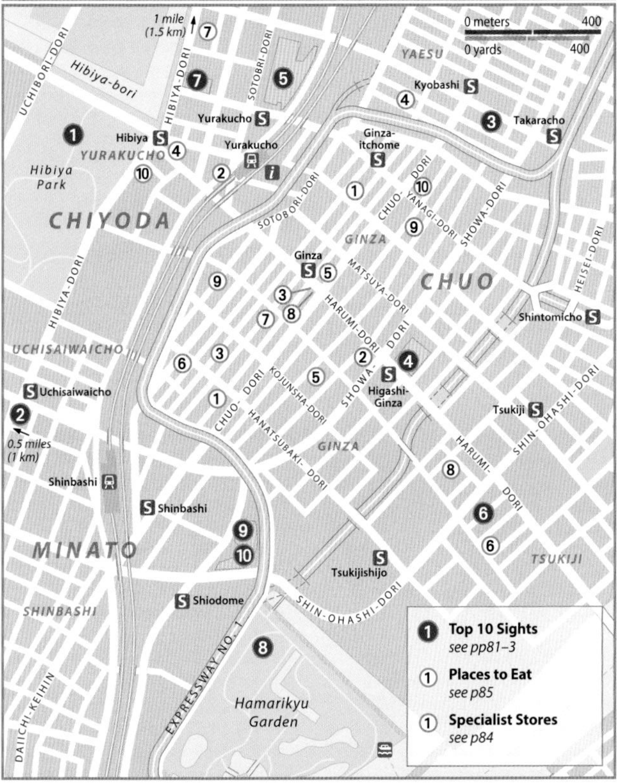

① Hibiya Park

MAP L4 ■ 1 Hibiyakoen, Chiyoda ■ 3501-6428

Built over a former military parade ground converted from the estates of shogun Ieyasu's less-favored Outer Lords, Hibiya Park was rebuilt as Japan's first Western-style park in 1903. European features, such as bandstands, a rose garden, an open-air theater, and a bronze heron fountain overlooked by a wisteria trellis, are set against a small but exquisite Japanese garden, with rock placements and cherry trees lining paths at the center of the park.

② Japan Sake and Shochu Information Center

MAP M4 ■ 1-16-15 Nishishinbashi, Minato ■ 3519-2091 ■ Open 10am–6pm Mon–Fri ■ www.japansake.or.jp/sake/en/jss/information-center

For those interested in knowing more about Japan's national beverage of sake and *shochu*, the center has a museum where visitors can sample 50 different types of sake, *shochu* and *awamori* (distilled rice liquor).

③ National Film Archive of Japan (NFAJ)

MAP N4 ■ 3-7-6 Kyobashi, Chuo ■ 5777-8600 ■ Opening times vary, check website for details ■ Adm ■ www.nfaj.go.jp/english

The only center in Japan devoted to the study and dissemination of Japanese and foreign films, the NFAJ holds almost 40,000 films in its collection, including many restored Japanese classics. Besides its two theaters, there is a library of books on film and a gallery featuring exhibitions of stills, photographs, and film-related items. The NFAJ sometimes runs programs of Japanese cinematic masterpieces, usually with English subtitles.

Inside National Film Archive of Japan

④ Kabuki-za Theater

MAP N5 ■ 4-12-15 Ginza, Chuo ■ 3545-6800 ■ www.kabukiweb.net/theatres/kabukiza

One of Ginza's most striking buildings is this theater devoted to the performing art of Kabuki. Rebuilt in recent years so that a soaring tower block could be added (in which is located a small museum), the theater's frontage features giant purple banners, lanterns, and colorful posters.

Flamboyant facade of Kabuki-za Theater

Interior of Tokyo International Forum

5 Tokyo International Forum

MAP M3 & M4 ■ 3-5-1 Marunouchi, Chiyoda ■ 5221-9000 ■ www.t-i-forum.co.jp/en

One of the city's architectural wonders, the majestic Tokyo International Forum was designed by Rafael Viñoly and completed in 1996. It functions as a premier culture convention center, with four graduated cubes encased in granite, abutting a high, tapering trajectory of glass and steel, aptly named Glass Hall. Crossing the sky-walks among the glass and girders at the transparent apex of the building, above cantilevered areas and atria, is like walking across a crystal suspended above the city.

6 Tsukiji Outer Market

MAP F6 ■ Tsukiji, Chuo

Even though the old fish market has departed for new premises in Toyosu, the old food businesses of the outer market remain and make for mouth-watering browsing. There are ample chances for grazing on street food, buying souvenirs, such as crockery, tea, and kitchen knives, and discovering Tsukiji Uogashi, the new center for food vendors.

7 Idemitsu Museum of Arts

MAP M3 ■ Teigeki Bldg, 9F, 3-1-1 Marunouchi, Chiyoda ■ 5777-8600 ■ Open 11am–5pm Tue–Sun (book ahead) ■ Adm ■ www.idemitsu-museum.or.jp/en

As petroleum tycoon Sazo Idemitsu's fortune increased, so did his passion for collecting Japanese and Asian art. Opened in 1966, the museum bearing his name displays a diverse, eclectic collection of artworks, which includes paintings, bronzes, ceramic ware, *ukiyo-e* prints, lacquer, and rare gold-painted screens. Its calligraphy holdings include the world's largest collection of works by the Zen monk Sengai. Works from China, Korea, and the Middle East are also periodically displayed. The room containing pottery shards affords tremendous ninth-floor views of the Imperial Palace grounds.

8 Hamarikyu Garden

MAP M6 ■ 1-1 Hamarikyu Teien, Chuo ■ Open 9am–5pm daily ■ Adm ■ www.tokyo-park.or.jp/teien/en/hama-rikyu

The younger brother of shogun Ietsuna had parts of the bay filled in and a villa built here in 1654. Completed by a later shogun, Ienari, the basic design and balance of the garden remain gloriously intact. The highlight is a large tidal pond, with a small tea pavilion, and islets connected by wooden bridges. Over 600 species of peony, in addition to crepe myrtle, cherry, iris, bamboo, and plum, grow in the garden today.

Tranquil Hamarikyu Garden

9 Shiodome and Caretta Shiodome

MAP M5 ■ 1-8-2 Higashishinbashi, Minato ■ 6218-2100

Resembling a futuristic mini-city, the bayside Shiodome features a grove of skyscrapers, notably Shiodome Media Tower and the highly regarded Conrad Tokyo hotel, as well as an Italian-style outdoor piazza, cafés, restaurants, and cocktail bars. The 47-story Caretta Shiodome houses more than 60 stores, restaurants, and cafés.

TAISHO CHIC

Popular culture thrived in Ginza during the Taisho period (1912–26), as a more liberal mood blew through the city. The age saw the appearance of the "Modern Girl," a product of European fashions, the American Jazz Age, and film divas. With their bobbed hair, these girls typified the confidence of a new age that challenged Japanese values.

10 Ad Museum Tokyo

MAP M5 ■ Caretta Shiodome, B1F-B2F, 1-8-2 Higashishinbashi, Minato ■ 6218-2500 ■ Open 11am–6pm Tue–Sat ■ www.admt.jp

Sponsored by advertising giant Dentsu in 2002, this spacious museum traces the history of Japanese advertising beginning from the Edo period to this day and age. It displays advertising publications and the exhibits run from colored woodblock prints to the latest TV commercials. The museum library has over 200,000 digitally saved advertisements.

A DAY SHOPPING IN GINZA

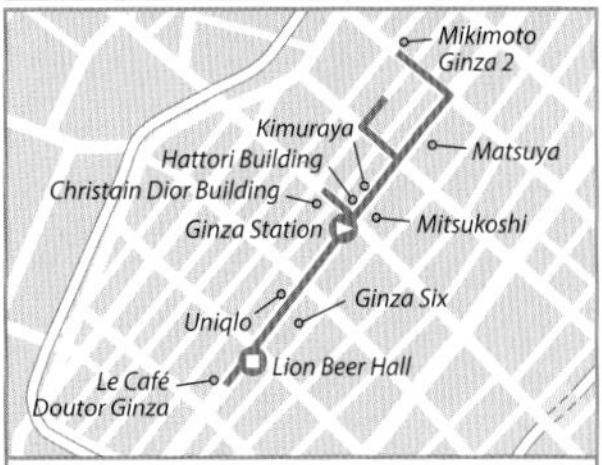

MORNING

Leave Ginza Station at the 4-chome exit well before 10am and have coffee at the elegant Le Café Doutor Ginza. Walk across to the **Mitsukoshi** *(4-6-16 Ginza)* department store opposite in time to be greeted by staff when it opens. Stroll a few steps to the svelte Christian Dior Building and then return to the 4-chome crossing. On the opposite corner, visit Wako, another department store. It is located in the **Hattori Building** *(see p41)*, a symbol of Ginza since the early 1930s. Next door, the bakery **Kimuraya** *(see p84)* has been specializing in *anpan*, a local delicacy, since 1869. Return to Mitsukoshi and browse its high-quality goods. Spare a few minutes to ascend to the roof, where offerings are left at a Shinto shrine to promote prosperity. Visit the food basement for a light lunch or green tea and Japanese sweets.

AFTERNOON

Cross the road and walk northeast along Chuo-dori, passing **Mikimoto Ginza 2** *(see p84)*, the originator of cultured pearls, and the department store Matsuya. Afterwards, visit some of the area's more recent retail entrants: the main Tokyo branch of fast-fashion retailer Uniqlo and, across the road, the plush **Ginza Six** *(see p66)* complex, which has a mix of luxury boutiques, contemporary art installations, and restaurants. Slake your thirst at the famous Lion Beer Hall nearby.

Specialist Stores

The quirky Mikimoto Ginza 2 building

1 Mikimoto Ginza 2

MAP N4 ■ 2-4-12 Ginza, Chuo ■ 3535-4611 ■ www.mikimoto.com

Housed in an eye-catching building designed by Toyo Ito, Mikimoto Ginza 2 sells the type of exquisite cultured pearls first developed by Kokichi Mikimoto in 1893.

2 Oonoya

MAP N5 ■ 5-12-3 Ginza, Chuo ■ 3541-0975

Founded in 1868, across from the Kabuki-za Theater, this store focuses on *tabi* socks and traditional patterned *tenugui* handkerchiefs.

3 Akebono

MAP M4 ■ 5-7-19 Ginza, Chuo ■ 3571-3640

The store specializes in *wagashi*, Japanese confections eaten with green tea, which are made from traditional ingredients such as *anko* (sweet red bean paste). Branches can be found in Tokyo's department stores.

4 Itoya

MAP N5 ■ 2-7-15 Ginza, Chuo ■ 3561-8311

Opened in 1904, and now spread across two swanky buildings, Itoya is all about stationery, writing tools, and desktop items.

5 Kimuraya

MAP M4 ■ 4-5-7 Ginza, Chuo ■ 3561-0091

Set up in the 1870s, Kimuraya is best known for *anpan*, bread rolls that are stuffed with red bean paste.

6 Takumi

MAP M5 ■ 8-4-2 Ginza, Chuo ■ 3571-2017

An interesting mix of folk crafts, ceramics, and traditional toys in a tasteful setting.

7 Ginza Natsuno

MAP M5 ■ 6-7-4 Ginza, Chuo ■ www.e-ohashi.com

A small store with a huge selection of chopsticks. Light and portable, they make ideal souvenirs.

8 Kyukyodo

MAP M4 ■ 5-7-4 Ginza, Chuo ■ 3571-4429

A famed Japanese paper specialist, Kyukyodo has been in the trade since the 17th century. Gift cards, paper boxes, and incense are also on sale.

9 Niwaka

MAP N4 ■ 2-8-3 Ginza, Chuo ■ 5159-1117

Original, custom-designed jewelry created by artisans in Kyoto workshops are a specialty here. The store also has a made-to-order service.

10 Tanagokoro

MAP N4 ■ 1-8-15 Ginza, Chuo ■ www.tanagokoro.com/english

Purveyors of *binchotan*, a high-quality charcoal. Placed in a room or bath water, it is said to have curative powers and can also act as a purifier, humidifier, and deodorizer.

Places to Eat

PRICE CATEGORIES
Price ranges are for dinner for one, with a drink. Lunchtime menus are usually less expensive.

¥ under ¥3,000 ¥¥ ¥3,000–¥8,000
¥¥¥ over ¥8,000

1 Kyubei

MAP M5 ■ 8-7-6 Ginza, Chuo ■ 3571-6523 ■ Closed Sun ■ ¥¥¥

The high temple of sushi, Kyubei offers an extraordinary eating experience, even if it breaks the bank.

2 Shin Hinomoto

MAP M4 ■ 2-4-4 Yurakucho, Chiyoda ■ Closed Sun ■ www.shin-hinomoto.com ■ ¥¥

Owned and run by a Brit, this traditional *izakaya* (Japanese pub) prides itself on excellent fish.

3 Kanetanaka-an

7-6-16, Ginza, Chuo ■ 3289-8822 ■ Closed Sun ■ ¥¥¥

Sample a refined *kaiseki* five-course banquet showcasing different aspects of Japanese cooking.

4 Ten-ichi

MAP F5 ■ 1-8-1 Yurakucho, Chiyoda ■ www.tenichi.co.jp ■ ¥¥¥

The Peninsula branch of this popular restaurant chain serves delectable tempura.

5 Maru

MAP M5 ■ 6-12-15 Ginza, Chuo ■ Closed Sun ■ www.maru-mayfont.jp/en ■ ¥¥¥

Chic Maru *(see p62)* is well-known for its affordable *kaiseki* courses and its delicious rice dishes. Join the locals and make the most of the continually popular prix fixe lunch.

Sophisticated interior at Maru

6 Tsukiji Sushi-sei

MAP N5 ■ 4-13-5 Tsukiji, Chuo ■ 3544-1919 ■ ¥¥

Follow the crowd and ask for the reliable *omakase* (chef's choice) at this traditional, Edo-style sushi chain.

7 Bird Land

MAP M4 ■ Tsukamoto Sozan Bldg, B1, 4-2-15 Ginza, Chuo ■ 5250-1081 ■ Closed Sun & Mon ■ ¥¥

Very popular for its fine-quality and fresh *yakitori* (grilled sticks of chicken seasoned with soy sauce), Bird Land also offers other succulent well-presented chicken dishes too.

8 RyuGin

MAP M4 ■ Tokyo Midtown Hibiya, 1-1-2 Yurakucho, Chiyoda ■ www.nihonryori-ryugin.com ■ ¥¥¥

At RyuGin *(see p63)*, acclaimed chef Seiji Yamamoto presents a remarkably innovative take on the traditional *kaiseki* format.

9 Sato Yosuke

MAP M4 ■ Deihonkan, 1F, 6-4-17 Ginza, Chuo ■ www.sato-yoske.co.jp/en ■ ¥

This restaurant serves handmade *inaniwa udon*, noodles that originate from the mountains of Akita Prefecture, with different side dishes.

10 Edogin

MAP N5 ■ 4-5-1 Tsukiji, Chuo ■ 3543-4401 ■ ¥¥

With fish served straight from tanks, the sushi here couldn't be fresher. Servings are plentiful in a no-frills setting.

See map on p80

TOP 10 Ueno, Asakusa, and Oshiage

Even in the 21st century, parts of northeastern Tokyo retain their old Edo *shitamachi* character. Ueno is home to museums, temples, and a cherry tree-filled park as well as a major train station. Dotted with religious sites, traditional restaurants, and a wide range of shops, Asakusa appeals as much to the gourmand as to the Buddhist acolyte. Across the Sumida River, Oshiage has a retro appeal despite the looming presence of the contemporary Tokyo Skytree.

Tokyo National Museum

Ueno Park in fall

1 Ueno Park

This wonderful park *(see pp20–21)* is an engaging mix of leisure and culture. Among the highlights are the Tokyo National Museum, contemporary Japanese and Western art galleries, a science museum, avenues of cherry trees, and the Toshogu Shrine – a fine historical monument. For visitors more interested in leisure activities, there are also restaurants, cafés, a zoo, and a huge pond divided into a boating area, conservation corner, and a magnificent lotus pond.

UENO, ASAKUSA, AND OSHIAGE

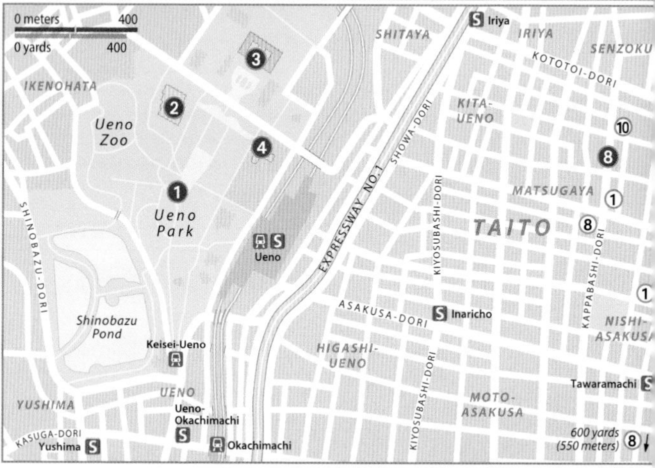

2 Tokyo Metropolitan Art Museum

MAP F1 ■ 8-36 Uenokoen, Taito ■ 3823-6921 ■ Open 9:30am–5:30pm daily except 1st & 3rd Mon of the month ■ Adm ■ www.tobikan.jp

Designed by architect Kunio Maekawa, this red-brick building has partially underground floors that may not be the perfect place to present art, but the exhibits are always interesting. The main hall shows an eclectic mix, ranging from Japanese flower arrangements and ink-brush works to contemporary installations.

3 Tokyo National Museum

This acclaimed museum *(see pp24–7)* is the centerpiece of Ueno Park. Its exhibits are divided between four main galleries: the Honkan displays a collection of Japanese arts and archeology; the Toyokan features arts and crafts from Asia, with an emphasis on Chinese, Central Asian, and Korean objects; the Heiseikan houses ancient archeological objects, including pottery and burial statues; and the Gallery of Horyu-ji Treasures is home to a permanent collection of precious religious artifacts. Also within the complex is the Hyokeikan, a fine example of Meiji-era architecture.

Museum of Nature and Science

4 National Museum of Nature and Science

MAP F1 ■ 7-20 Uenokoen, Taito ■ 3822-0111 ■ Open 9am–5pm Tue–Sun (to 8pm Fri & Sat) ■ Adm ■ www.kahaku.go.jp

A giant whale model outside the building announces this enormous museum, which is divided into the original, renovated section and a newer annex. Older displays and exhibits of dinosaurs, asteroids, and a reconstructed house made from mammoth tusks vie with modern touch-screen panels and models.

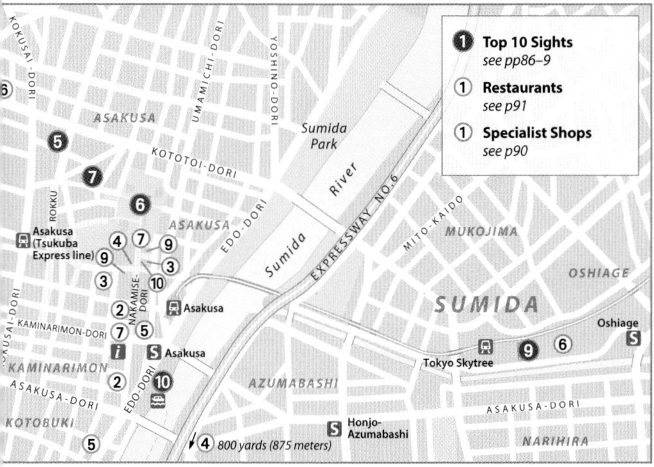

Edo Taito Traditional Crafts Center

RICKSHAWS

The *jinrikisha* (rickshaw) is said to have been invented in Japan in 1869. Yosuke Izumi's workshop produced the prototype, a great transportation innovation in Tokyo's narrow roads. Four years later, there were over 34,000 registered rickshaws in the city, still a common sight until World War II. Beautifully lacquered rickshaws have made a comeback in tourist spots such as Asakusa. Expect to pay around ¥5,000 for a 15-minute ride.

5 Edo Taito Traditional Crafts Center

MAP R2 ■ 2-22-13 Asakusa, Taito ■ 3842-1990 ■ Open 10am–6pm daily ■ Closed 2nd & 4th Tue of the month

This museum was set up to preserve and promote local craft industries and techniques dating from the Edo period. Over 250 displays represent 50 different traditional crafts, with demonstrations on weekends.

6 Senso-ji Temple

Tokyo's mother temple *(see pp14–15)* looms majestically at the end of Nakamise-dori, an avenue of stores selling souvenirs and snacks. Two imposing gates lead to the great incense burner standing before the cavernous main hall, designed in a style known as *gongen-zukuri*. Within the same compound, Asakusa Shrine was founded in 1649 and rebuilt several times. Erected even earlier, the nearby 1618 Niten-mon gate remains completely intact, a miraculous survivor of earthquakes, typhoons, and air raids.

7 Hanayashiki

MAP R1 ■ 2-28-1 Asakusa, Taito ■ 3842-8780 ■ Open 10am–6pm daily ■ Adm ■ www.hanayashiki.net

Once part of an aristocratic residence to the west of Senso-ji Temple, the Hanayashiki gardens were opened in the Asakusa Rokku entertainment district in 1853. An Asakusa institution, this amusement park retains its retro quality, with old-fashioned game machines that complement an eerily realistic ghost house dating from the 1950s and Japan's oldest rollercoaster.

Hozo-mon Gate at Senso-ji Temple

8 Kappabashi Kitchenware Town

MAP Q2 ■ Kappabashi-dori, Taito

A long street, Kappabashi-dori is known by its sobriquet, "Kitchen Town." The 170 stores here sell plastic food samples for window displays, chef outfits, chopsticks, ceramics, and pots and pans. It's a delight for both professional and amateur chefs.

9 Tokyo Skytree

MAP H2 ■ 1-1-2 Oshiage, Sumida ■ 0570-55-0634 ■ Open 10am–9pm daily ■ Adm (for observation decks only) ■ www.tokyo-skytree.jp

Opened in 2012, the 2,080-ft (634-m) Tokyo Skytree has two observation decks. Although the architect sought to create a futuristic building, several traditional Japanese elements went into its design. Even the color is based on the traditional Japanese blueish-white color called *aijiro*.

Tokyo Skytree dominates the skyline

10 Water Buses

Cruise boats ply the Sumida River *(see pp16–17)*, offering a different perspective of the capital and connecting several attractions that make for a fun day out. Tokyo Cruise is the most popular operator *(see p123)*. After visiting Senso-ji Temple, take a boat from Asakusa down the river to Hamarikyu Garden, before continuing on to the human-made island of Odaiba, which is packed with family-friendly attractions.

A DAY IN OLD ASAKUSA

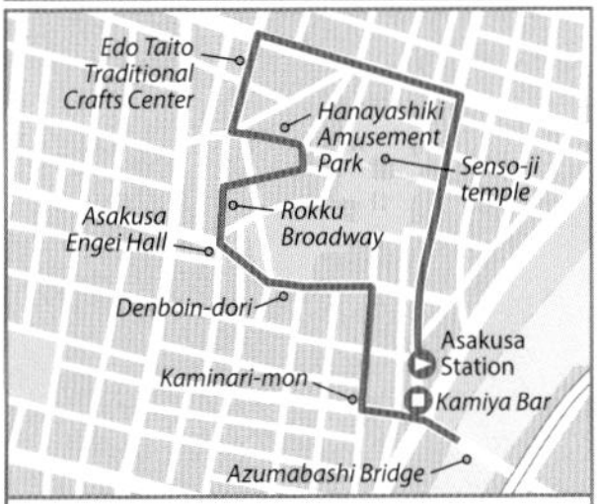

MORNING

Exit Asakusa Station, walk north along Umamichi-dori to Kototoi-dori. Turn left and the **Edo Taito Traditional Crafts Center** is a short walk away. The nearby **Hanayashiki** Amusement Park is a relic of the old entertainment district of Rokku. Southwest of Hanayashiki stretches the Rokku Broadway, a pedestrian street that still has a few traditional theaters as well as comedy and story-telling halls, including **Asakusa Engei Hall** *(see p59)*. Stop to look at the street performers, posters and lively barkers outside on Rokku Broadway. The narrow backstreets around Denboin-dori have many cheap, but characterful, restaurants serving fried noodles, *yakitori*, and *oden*, a fish-cake hot pot.

AFTERNOON

Walk south to the great **Kaminari-mon** *(see p14)*, the main entrance to **Senso-ji temple** *(see pp14–15)* to admire the giant paper lantern and the ancient guardian statues. Walk toward the **Sumida River** *(see pp16–17)* and the station where you began. Before getting to the river, stop by **Kamiya Bar** *(see p64)*, the city's oldest Western-style pub. From mid-morning, waistcoated waiters serve the bar's trademark *denki-bran*, a heady brandy-based concoction. Finish the day by catching a water bus, from next to the brightly painted Azumabashi Bridge, down the river to Hamarikyu Garden or Odaiba.

See map on p86–7

Specialist Shops

Shoppers enjoy some retail therapy at Solamachi

1 Ganso

MAP Q2 ■ 3-7-6 Nishiasakusa, Taito ■ Open 10am–5:30pm daily ■ www.ganso-sample.com

This store on Kappabashi-dori sells *sanpuru*, the fake plastic food seen in many Japanese restaurant windows.

2 Bunsendo

MAP R3 ■ 1-30-1 Asakusa, Taito ■ 3844-9711 ■ Open 10:30am–4:30pm daily (to 5pm Sat & Sun)

The specialty here are the folding fans used by Japanese dancers, Kabuki actors, and geisha.

3 Fujiya

MAP R2 ■ 2-2-15 Asakusa, Taito ■ 3841-2283 ■ Open 11am–5pm Fri–Wed

Tenugui (printed cotton towels) make great practical souvenirs, and this store has hundreds of designs.

4 Ojima

MAP R2 ■ 2-3-2 Asakusa, Taito ■ 4285-9664 ■ Open 9am–5pm daily ■ www.edokiriko.jp

Ojima is the place to buy delicate Edo Kiriko glassware, with engraved patterns on colored glass.

5 Kurodaya

MAP R3 ■ 1-2-5 Asakusa, Taito ■ 3844-7511 ■ Open 10am–6pm Tue–Sun

This store specializes in *washi* (Japanese paper), woodblock prints, and other paper novelties.

6 Solamachi

MAP H2 ■ 1-1-2 Oshiage, Sumida ■ Open 10am–9pm daily ■ www.tokyo-solamachi.jp

Sushi-shaped fridge magnets, incense, decorative fans, chopsticks, and anime merchandise are sold in this large mall beneath Tokyo Skytree.

7 Sukeroku

MAP R2 ■ 2-3-1 Asakusa, Taito ■ 3844-0577 ■ Open 10am–6pm daily

Established in 1866, this is the only store in the city that makes and sells miniature Edo-style dolls and toys.

8 Maito Design Works

MAP G2 ■ 4-10-12 Kuramae, Taito ■ Open 11:30am–6:30pm Tue–Sun ■ www.maitokomuro.com

In the fashionable Kuramae district, this store specializes in items made using traditional *kusakizome* dyeing.

9 Yonoya Kushiho

MAP R3 ■ 1-37-10 Asakusa, Taito ■ 3844-1755 ■ Open 10:30am–5pm Thu–Tue

The place to come for great-quality boxwood combs, hair, and *netsuke* ornaments since 1717.

10 Soi

MAP Q2 ■ 3-25-11 Nishiasakusa, Taito ■ 6802-7732 ■ Open noon–5pm Mon–Fri, 11am–6pm Sat & Sun

Located on Kappabashi-dori, this is one of Tokyo's best homeware shops, with a great selection of ceramics.

→ *See map on p86–7*

Restaurants

PRICE CATEGORIES
Price ranges are for dinner for one, with a drink. Lunchtime menus are usually less expensive.

¥ under ¥3,000 ¥¥ ¥3,000–¥8,000
¥¥¥ over ¥8,000

1 Sometaro
MAP Q3 ■ 2-2-2 Nishiasakusa, Taito ■ 3844-9502 ■ ¥

The only dish served here is *okonomiyaki* – pancakes made with shrimp, octopus, and vegetables.

2 Namiki Yabu Soba
MAP R3 ■ 2-11-9 Kaminarimon, Taito ■ 3841-1340 ■ Closed Thu ■ ¥

This ever-popular *soba* (buckwheat noodle) store is located just up the road from Senso-ji Temple.

3 Daikokuya
MAP R3 ■ 1-38-10 Asakusa, Taito ■ 3844-1111 ■ ¥¥

Expect long lines for the delicious fish and vegetable tempura dishes at this popular restaurant.

4 Kappo Yoshiba
MAP H3 ■ 2-14-5 Yokoami, Sumida ■ Closed Sun ■ www.kapou-yoshiba.jp/english ■ ¥¥

Housed in a former sumo-training stable, this is an atmospheric restaurant. It serves great *chanko nabe* – sumo wrestlers' favorite hotpot.

5 Komakata Dozeu
MAP R2 ■ 1-7-12 Komagata, Taito ■ 3842-4001 ■ ¥¥

Grilled and stewed loach, a small fish resembling an eel, has been served in time-honored fashion at this restaurant since it opened in 1801.

6 Otafuku
MAP Q2 ■ 1-6-2 Senzoku, Taito ■ 3871-2521 ■ Closed Mon ■ ¥¥

This charming century-old restaurant specializes in *oden*, items such as scallops, fish cake, boiled egg, and chunks of radish simmered in a broth.

7 Maguro Bito
MAP R3 ■ 2-18-12 Kaminarimon, Taito ■ 3847-7139 ■ ¥¥

Expect great value for money from this popular *kaitenzushi* (conveyor belt sushi) restaurant, where the specialty is *maguro* (tuna).

8 Asakusa Imahan
MAP Q2 ■ 3-1-12 Nishiasakusa, Taito ■ www.asakusaimahan.co.jp ■ ¥¥

This restaurant specializes in *shabu-shabu* and *sukiyaki*. The former consists of wafer-thin cuts of beef cooked in a boiling broth, while the latter is beef and vegetables prepared in a sweet, soy-based sauce.

Asakusa Imahan's traditional interior

9 Waentei-Kikko
MAP R2 ■ 2-2-13 Asakusa, Taito ■ Closed Wed ■ www.waentei-kikko.com ■ ¥¥

Refined Japanese cuisine is offered in an informal setting at this venue. Enjoy a *shamisen* (Japanese banjo) recital while you dine.

10 Yoroiya
MAP H2 ■ 1-36-7 Asakusa, Taito ■ 3845-4618 ■ ¥

This lively ramen restaurant serves excellent *shoyu-ramen* (made with a soy-based soup), and delicious gyoza dumplings.

Following pages *Red* torii *(gates) at Hie Shrine*

平成九年十二月十五日

日枝神社奉賛会

TOP 10 Roppongi and Akasaka

Detail of the exterior of Nogi Shrine

Roppongi is a major center for the arts, shopping, communications, and lifestyle, and it is Tokyo's premier nightlife district. Here, you will find innovative centers and facilities, including Roppongi Hills and Tokyo Midtown. Nearby, Akasaka is a business district on the doorstep of Japan's parliament and government offices. It is home to numerous bars and restaurants as well as some important temples and shrines.

1 Roppongi Hills

MAP D6 ■ 6-10-1 Roppongi, Minato ■ www.roppongihills.com

Opened in 2003, this sprawling city-within-a-city includes gardens and a live-performance area. The central structure, the 54-story Mori Tower, houses offices, more than 200 stores, restaurants, bars, the Grand Hyatt hotel, and the Mori Art Museum.

Roppongi Hills, a lively complex

ROPPONGI AND AKASAKA

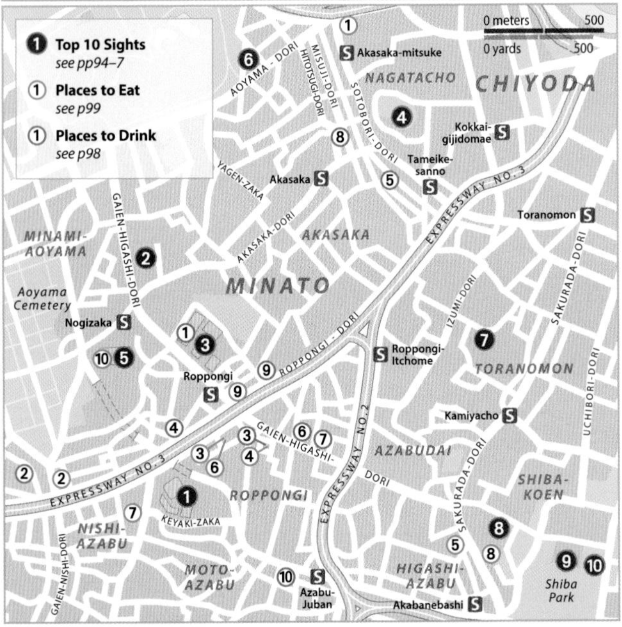

2 Nogi Shrine

MAP C5 ■ 8-11-27 Akasaka, Minato ■ 3478-3001 ■ www.nogijinja.or.jp/english

This modest but significant shrine honors General Maresuke Nogi, who, along with his wife, committed ritual suicide on September 13, 1912 in an act of loyalty when Emperor Meiji died. The event divided the country into those who admired the act as a heroic gesture, and those who condemned it as an archaic practice. The general's house stands beside the shrine and is open on the eve and anniversary of the couple's death.

3 Tokyo Midtown

MAP D5 ■ 9-7-1 Akasaka, Minato ■ www.tokyo-midtown.com

Unveiled in 2007, the Tokyo Midtown development set aside 40 per cent of the complex for Hinokicho Park and Midtown Garden. Midtown Tower and its core of buildings contain offices, apartments, shops, bars, restaurants, and the Ritz-Carlton Tokyo hotel. The area's cultural credentials are enhanced by the superb Suntory Museum of Art *(see p47)* and 21_21 Design Sight, a design gallery conceived by architect Tadao Ando and fashion guru Issey Miyake.

4 Hie Shrine

MAP J4 ■ 2-10-5 Nagatacho, Chiyoda ■ 3581-2471 ■ www.hiejinja.net

Burned down in the air raids of 1945 and rebuilt in 1958, Hie Shrine was originally erected as a protective shrine. Its role of deflecting evil spirits from Edo Castle is seen in wood carvings to the left of the main shrine, depicting a monkey protectively holding a baby. Pregnant women come here to pray for safe deliveries, and the biannual festival Sanno Matsuri – a procession celebrating the imperial family – begins and ends at the shrine.

National Art Center's grand interior

5 National Art Center, Tokyo

MAP C6 ■ 7-22-2 Roppongi, Minato ■ 5777-8600 ■ Open 10am–6pm Wed–Mon ■ Adm ■ www.nact.jp

Japan's largest exhibition space, the National Art Center, Tokyo hosts temporary exhibitions, such as Nitten, an annual event highlighting Japanese and Western painting, sculpture, craftwork, and calligraphy. Built in 2007, the space features an undulating glass facade, slated walls, and a wooden floor.

Atmospheric Hie Shrine

Statues of foxes stand guard at Toyokawa Inari Betsuin

6 Toyokawa Inari Betsuin

MAP D5 ■ 1-4-7 Motoakasaka, Minato ■ 3408-3414

A Zen temple with Shinto elements, the Toyokawa is distinctive for its orange banners, lanterns, and hundreds of statues of foxes representing the bodhisattva Jizo (protector of children and travelers), and Kannon, (the Goddess of Mercy). Behind the main buildings are forest-like paths lined with *senbon nobori* streamers hung by devotees in the hope of fulfilling their wishes.

7 Musée Tomo

MAP K5 ■ Nishi-Kubo Bldg, 4-1-35 Toranomon, Minato ■ 5733-5131 ■ Open 11am–6pm Tue–Sun ■ Adm ■ www.musee-tomo.or.jp

Established in 2003 by Tomo Kikuchi, a collector of contemporary ceramics, this small museum is one of the most elegant in Tokyo. Exhibitions change every few months, highlighting a particular craftsperson or a school of ceramic ware, such as Bizen or Raku.

ROPPONGI STREET ART

Many world-class artists were asked to create works on and around Roppongi Hills. Louise Bourgeois's huge spider sculpture, *Maman*, is the most visible, but there are also wall drawings, an illuminated robot, a giant coffee bean installation, digital screen models, a 3-D landscape painting, and waveform furniture such as benches.

8 Tokyo Tower

MAP K6 ■ 4-2-8 Shibakoen, Minato ■ 3433-5111 ■ Times vary, check website ■ www.tokyotower.co.jp/en

When it opened in 1958, this broadcasting mast was the tallest building in Tokyo. Despite its age, it attracts crowds of visitors spurred by nostalgia and the views from its observation decks. It's showing signs of modernizing, too, with a new e-sports center having opened in 2022 in the restaurant-filled complex at its base.

Tokyo Tower against the sky

9 Zojo-ji Temple

MAP E6 ■ 4-7-35 Shibakoen, Minato ■ 3432-1431 ■ Open 9am–5pm daily ■ www.zojoji.or.jp/en

Another victim of World War II air raids, Zojo-ji Temple is a 1970s ferro-concrete reconstruction. The original temple was founded in 1393 and then removed to its present location, close to Tokyo Tower, in 1598. In the next century, it was chosen by the Tokugawa shoguns as their ancestral temple. Today, the temple hosts many religious events. The main hall contains ancient statues, written *sutras*, and other sacred objects, while the Ankokuden hall holds the Black Image of Amida Buddha, known as a miracle-working buddha that gives victory and defends against evil.

Ankokuden hall, Zojo-ji Temple

10 San-mon Gate

MAP E6 ■ Shibakoen, Minato

Fires and earthquakes have been reducing Tokyo's buildings to rubble for over 400 years, but the beautiful San-mon Gate, the main entrance to Zojo-ji Temple, has remained miraculously intact. The oldest wooden structure in the city, it was erected in 1622. The three tiers of the red-lacquered gate, an Important Cultural Treasure, represent the three stages required to enter Nirvana. The gate looks especially attractive at night, when it is illuminated.

A DAY IN THE ART TRIANGLE

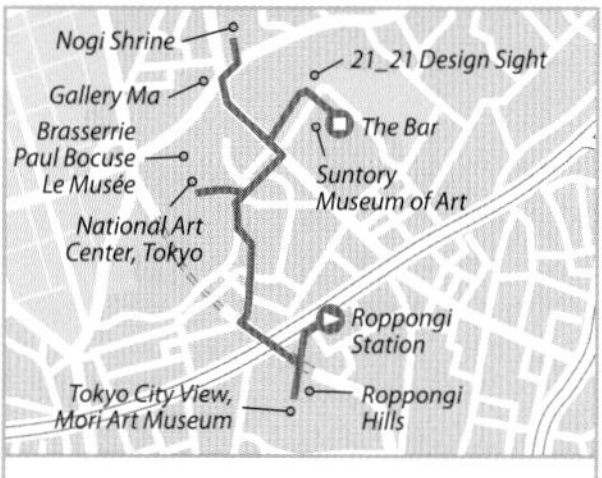

MORNING

Leave Roppongi Station by Exit 1C, which leads directly into **Roppongi Hills** *(see p94)*; at the top of the escalator is Louise Bourgeouis's *Maman*, a giant sculpture of a spider and one of many pieces of public art surrounding the shopping and business complex. Head to the top of Mori Tower for the excellent **Mori Art Museum** *(see p45)* and the urban vistas of the Tokyo City View observation deck. Cross Roppongi-dori and walk north to the **National Art Center, Tokyo** *(see p95)*, a huge 12-room art venue where you can view an eclectic mix of art, displayed as part of a changing program of temporary exhibitions. You can also dine here at **Brasserie Paul Bocuse Le Musée** *(see p99)*, set atop a massive inverted concrete cone. Take time to admire the views before setting off again.

AFTERNOON

Head north in the direction of **Nogi Shrine** *(see p95)*, and then visit Gallery Ma. Sponsored by the bathroom appliance and fixtures company Toto, its exhibitions focus mainly on architecture and the latest trends in design. The gallery also has an excellent bookstore. Retrace your steps toward Roppongi Crossing to find **Tokyo Midtown** *(see p95)*, where you can check out what's showing at either the Suntory Museum of Art or the **21_21 Design Sight** *(see p49)*. **The Bar** *(see p98)*, located on Midtown's 45th floor, is the ideal spot for a cocktail after a day of sightseeing.

See map on p94

Places to Drink

1 The Bar

MAP D5 ■ 9-7-1 Akasaka, Minato ■ www.tokyomidtown.com

Situated in the Ritz Carlton on Tokyo Midtown's 45th floor, this glamorous cocktail bar has an extensive drinks menu and incredible views.

2 These

MAP C6 ■ 2-15-12 Nishiazabu, Minato ■ www.these-jp.com

Stocked with books, this cocktail bar almost feels like a library – albeit one with a great selection of spirits.

3 BrewDog

MAP U4 ■ 5-3-2 Roppongi, Minato ■ www.brewdog.com/uk/bars/global/Roppongi

With 22 craft beers on tap, BrewDog is an ideal place to try Japanese and European brews.

4 Agave Clover

MAP T4 ■ DM Bldg B1F, 7-18-11 Roppongi, Minato ■ 3497-0229 ■ Closed Sun & Mon

An expensive cantina-style drinking hole, with over 500 varieties of tequila.

5 The Pink Cow

MAP D5 ■ 2-7-5 Akasaka, Minato ■ Closed Sun ■ www.thepinkcow.com

A favorite with expats, this lively bar and gallery is good for cocktails and California-Mexican food.

6 Propaganda

MAP U4 ■ Yua Roppongi Bldg 2F, 3-14-9 Roppongi, Minato ■ 3423-0988 ■ Closed Sun ■ www.propaganda6.tokyo

Popular and loud, this chic and well-stocked shot bar has English-speaking staff.

7 Hobgoblin

MAP U4 ■ Aoba Roppongi Bldg 1F, 3-16-33 Roppongi, Minato ■ 3568-1280 ■ www.hobgoblin.jp

This English pub serves decent ale and British pub grub, such as bangers and mash and shepherd's pie.

8 Gen Yamamoto

MAP D6 ■ 1-6-4 Azabu-Juban, Minato ■ Closed Mon ■ www.genyamamoto.jp

This tiny bar, with just eight seats at the counter, is known for making some of Tokyo's most inventive cocktails. The tasting menu features blends of seasonal fruit and fine liquors.

9 Cask Strength

MAP D6 ■ 3-9-11 Roppongi, Minato ■ www.cask-s.com

Grab a seat at this old-fashioned whiskey bar, which deals in local and rare tipples.

10 Codename Mixology

MAP D5 ■ 3-14-3 Akasaka, Minato ■ 6459-1129

Elegant interiors, low lighting, and innovative cocktails all define this cool bar.

Plush interiors of Codename Mixology

Places to Eat

PRICE CATEGORIES

Price ranges are for dinner for one, with a drink. Lunchtime menus are usually less expensive.

¥ under ¥3,000 ¥¥ ¥3,000–¥8,000 ¥¥¥ over ¥8,000

1 Ninja Tokyo

MAP D4 ■ 2-14-3 Nagatacho ■ www.ninja-tokyo.jp/home/home-en ■ ¥¥¥

This fun ninja-themed restaurant, designed to look like a feudal fortress, serves *kaiseki*-style courses.

2 Gonpachi

MAP C6 ■ 1-13-11 Nishi-Azabu, Minato ■ www.gonpachi.jp/nishi-azabu ■ ¥¥

Styled like an old Edo inn, this restaurant was used for a fight scene in the movie *Kill Bill*. The specialty is *sumiyaki*, charcoal-grilled skewers.

3 Fukuzushi

MAP U5 ■ 6-5-24 Roppongi, Minato ■ 3402-4116 ■ ¥¥¥

Beside the usual tuna and squid offerings are the less common shad, conger eel, and other delicacies at this no-frills sushi restaurant.

4 Inakaya Roppongi

MAP U4 ■ 3-14-7 Roppongi, Minato ■ 3408-5040 ■ ¥¥¥

An old-fashioned *robatayaki* (grilled food) restaurant, offering all manner of meat and other foods.

5 Nodaiwa

MAP V5 ■ 1-5-4 Higashiazabu, Minato ■ 3583-7852 ■ Closed Sun ■ ¥¥

Specializing in wild eel, Nodaiwa serves charcoal-grilled fish drizzled with an appetizing sauce.

6 Hassan

MAP T4 ■ 6-1-20 Roppongi, Minato ■ 3403-8333 ■ ¥¥¥

The star course here is the all-you-can-eat dinner of *shabu-shabu*, thin cuts of beef dipped in a boiling broth.

7 Chinese Café Eight

MAP T5 ■ Court Annexe, 3-2-13 Nishiazabu, Minato ■ www.en.cceight.com ■ ¥¥

This fun, informal 24-hour café attracts a young crowd. The specialties here are Peking Duck and dim sum.

8 Tofuya-Ukai

MAP W5 ■ 4-4-13 Shibakoen, Minato ■ Closed 3rd Mon ■ www.ukai.co.jp/shiba ■ ¥¥¥

Gorgeous *kaiseki*-style meals, made up of tofu and seasonal ingredients, are served in this beautiful old wooden building.

Garden views at Tofuya-Ukai

9 Ippudo

MAP T4 ■ 4-9-11 Roppongi, Minato ■ 5775-7561 ■ ¥

You may have to wait in line to get in, but Ippudo's ramen is worth the wait. Slippery *soba* noodles in a creamy *tonkotsu* (pork bone) soup and *gyoza* (fried dumplings) are recommended.

10 Brasserie Paul Bocuse Le Musée

MAP T4 ■ 3F National Arts Center, 7-22-2 Roppongi, Minato ■ 5770-8161 ■ Closed Tue ■ ¥¥

Located inside the striking National Arts Center building, this stylish restaurant serves light French cuisine. The fixed-price lunches are extremely popular.

See map on p94

TOP 10 Aoyama, Harajuku, and Shibuya

Omotesando-dori, the chic boulevard running through Aoyama and Omotesando, is Tokyo's fashion quarter. A shift in mood occurs as Omotesando segues into Harajuku and Takeshita-dori; the latter is a street humming with off-the-peg boutiques, street stalls, fast-food joints, and a young crowd. Giant video screens characterize Shibuya, which is crammed with fashion and department stores, clubs, museums, art galleries, and cafés.

Stylish interior of the Nezu Museum

1 Nezu Museum

MAP C6 ■ 6-5-1 Minamiaoyama, Minato ■ 3400-2536 ■ Open 10am–5pm Tue–Sun ■ Adm ■ www.nezu-muse.or.jp

This museum was established by the family of Meiji-era tycoon and politician Kaichiro Nezu after his death. Some of the collection's textiles, lacquerware, and ceramics are so rare they are registered as National Treasures. The most famous piece is Ogata Korin's screen painting *Irises*.

AOYAMA, HARAJUKU, AND SHIBUYA

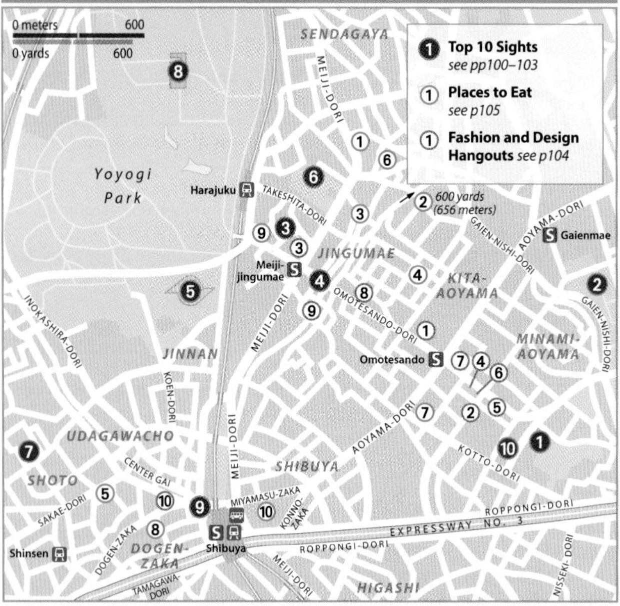

Cherry blossoms as seen in spring, Aoyama Cemetery

2 Aoyama Cemetery

MAP C5 ■ 2-32-2 Minamiaoyama, Minato

The graves of John Manjiro, the first Japanese person to go to America in the early 19th century, and Professor Ueno, the owner of the faithful dog Hachiko immortalized in bronze outside Shibuya Station, are here. Japan's first public cemetery explodes into clouds of pink petals each spring, when crowds of people visit for *hanami* (cherry blossom) viewing parties.

3 Ota Memorial Museum of Art

MAP B5 ■ 1-10-10 Jingumae, Shibuya ■ 050-5541-8600 ■ Open 10:30am–5:30pm Tue–Sun ■ Adm ■ www.ukiyoe-ota-muse.jp/eng

This remarkable museum has Tokyo's finest collection of *ukiyo-e* woodblock prints – about 14,000. The great names in this genre, such as Hiroshige, Utamaro, Hokusai, and Sharaku, all feature here. The collection was begun by Seizo Ota, a wealthy businessman who realized that many of the best works were being sold to foreign museums.

4 Omotesando

MAP R4

Even if you're not interested in shopping at the rows of designer boutiques here, strolling the length of tree-lined Omotesando is a pleasure, not least for its exceptional collection of contemporary buildings. There are buildings by nearly all of Japan's winners of the prestigious Pritzker Prize, including Tadao Ando (Omotesando Hills and Collezione), Kazuyo Sejima and Ryue Nishizawa of SANAA (Dior Building), and Toyo Ito (Tod's). It's also a great place for people-watching, particularly near Harajuku Station.

Taking a stroll down Omotesando

5 Yoyogi National Gymnasium

MAP Q4 ■ 2-1-1 Jinnan, Shibuya ■ 3468-1171

A residential compound for American personnel during the Occupation (1945–52), the park area was called "Washington Heights." The Japanese government requested its return, turning the site into the Olympic Village in 1964 for the Tokyo Games. Architect Kenzo Tange designed the sweeping roofs of the pavilions at the southern end which still look modern.

Stylish Yoyogi National Gymnasium

6 Takeshita-dori and Togo Shrine

MAP B5 ■ Jingumae 1, Shibuya

On weekends, narrow Takeshita-dori is probably the single-most crowded spot in the entire city. The home of subculture kitsch, the lane is packed with theme clothing stores, takeout food, crêpe stands, and stores selling character items, cuddly toys, and all manner of quirky accessories. Just a few steps behind the street are the serenely quiet precincts of Togo Shrine. Dedicated to Admiral Heihachiro Togo, who engineered the defeat of the Russian fleet in 1905, the grounds offer a soothing escape from the heaving masses of Takeshita-dori.

7 Toguri Museum of Art

MAP A6 ■ 1-11-3 Shoto, Shibuya ■ 3465-0070 ■ Open 10am–5pm Wed–Sun (to 8pm Fri & Sat) ■ Adm ■ www.toguri-museum.or.jp

This small museum in a leafy residential area has an outstanding collection of Oriental porcelain. The Japanese collection includes fine examples of Imari and Nabeshima wares; the Chinese pieces represent the Tang, Song, and later dynasties. The highlight of the Korean section are fine Goryeo-era pieces.

8 Meiji Jingu Shrine

A massive gate, Ichi no Torii, marks the main entrance to the forested compound and outer grounds of Meiji Jingu Shrine *(see pp30–31)*. Broadleaf trees and shrubs are planted beside gravel paths leading to the shrine. Burned to cinders in World War II, the current 1958 building is a faithful reproduction of the original shrine dedicated to Emperor Meiji, who died in 1912.

Visitors gather in front of the main Meiji Jingu Shrine building

Crowds at Shibuya Crossing

9 Shibuya Crossing

MAP Q6

Shibuya Station is undergoing a major redevelopment, which has resulted in the completion of the Shibuya Hikarie complex on the east side. But it's the crossing at the station's northwest corner that is the most famous sight here: the flow of people on the move surrounded by a blaze of neon and video screens is mesmerizing. Look for the statue and mural of the faithful dog Hachiko amid the crowds lingering in front of the station.

SHIBUYA STYLE

Shibuya is one of the major centers of street fashion in Tokyo and there have been many subculture trends that originated here. The iconic Shibuya 109 building, visible from Shibuya Crossing, offers some of the hottest brands as well as new and upcoming trends. A good place for noticing what young Japan likes to wear is Center Gai, a lively alley near Shibuya Crossing with popular stores, nightclubs, and fast food joints.

10 Taro Okamoto Memorial Museum

MAP C6 ■ 6-1-19 Minamiaoyama, Minato ■ 3406-0801 ■ Open 10am–6pm Wed–Mon ■ Adm ■ www.taro-okamoto.or.jp

The former studio of the famed Japanese artist Taro Okamoto (1911–1996), sometimes referred to as the Japanese Picasso, is now a museum. Founded in 1998 by his adopted daughter Toshiko, it re-creates the atmosphere of the artist's atelier.

A DAY OF ARCHITECTURE

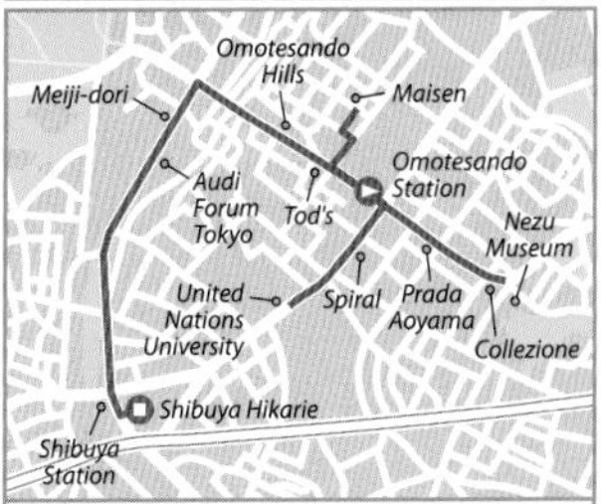

MORNING

After exiting Omotesando Station, stroll down Aoyama-dori until you see the open plaza outside the United Nations University on your right, designed by Kenzo Tange. Turn back the way you came until you glimpse **Spiral** *(see p46)* on the right. Return to the intersection at the subway and follow the road on the right up to the triangular outline of **Prada Aoyama** *(see p51)*. A little farther on, Collezione is the work of the self-taught architect, Tadao Ando. Kengo Kuma's design for the **Nezu Museum** *(see p100)* is at the southern end of **Omotesando** *(see p101)*. Return to the station area and head into the streets east of Omotesando to find the *tonkatsu* (pork cutlet) restaurant **Maisen** *(see p105)*.

AFTERNOON

The stretch of Omotesando heading towards Meiji-dori is lined with impressive architecture, including the building for the leather goods store Tod's, designed by Toyo Ito, and **Omotesando Hills** *(see p104)*, a fashion brand complex with cool lines and angles. Take a left on Meiji-dori; a little farther on you can see the glass sections and counter-angles of a 2008 building called the Iceberg, originally home to the Audi Forum. Walk on to Shibuya Station, which is in the process of being redeveloped with new towers. One that has been completed is Shibuya Hikarie – its Sky Lobby on the 11th floor has great views and you can dine at d47 Shokudo in the complex.

See map on p100 ←

Fashion and Design Hangouts

1 Anniversaire Café

MAP S5 ■ 3-5-30 Kitaaoyama, Minato ■ 5411-5988

A terrace seat here doesn't come cheap, but this chic café is the place to see and be seen.

2 BAPE Exclusive

MAP S5 ■ 5-5-8 Minamiaoyama, Minato ■ 3407-2145

Bathing Ape (BAPE) is one of Tokyo's most original fashion stores. The distinctive jeans and hoodies attract a very cool, discerning crowd.

3 Laforet Harajuku

MAP R4 ■ 1-11-6 Jingumae, Shibuya ■ www.laforet.ne.jp/en

The alternative styles offered by hundreds of clothes and accessory stores here attract teens. It's also a wonderful place to observe Tokyo's youthful fashion fads.

4 Comme des Garçons

MAP S5 ■ 5-2-1 Minamiaoyama, Minato ■ 3406-3951

Curving glass windows and tilted walls hint at the creative approach to fashion here at Rei Kawakubo's main fashion store.

Showroom, Comme des Garçons

5 Undercover

MAP S5 ■ Bleu Cinq Point Bldg, 5-3-22 Minamiaoyama, Minato ■ www.undercoverism.com

The brainchild of former punk musician Jun Takahashi, this store sells youth streetwear.

Prada Aoyama's amazing storefront

6 Prada Aoyama

MAP S5 ■ 5-2-6 Minamiaoyama, Minato ■ 6418-0400

Prada's quality, chic offerings are almost overshadowed by the brilliance of this crystal-like building.

7 Homme Plisse Issey Miyake

MAP S5 ■ 3-18-14 Minamiaoyama, Minato ■ 3423-1408

The flagship store for men stylishly presents Miyake's highly original approach to fashion.

8 Omotesando Hills

MAP R4 ■ 4-12-10 Jingumae, Shibuya ■ www.omotesandohills.com

Boutiques, such as Jimmy Choo, and specialist stores, including e.m. jewelry, vie with other brands here.

9 Cat Street

MAP B5 ■ Omotesando, Minato

This quiet fashion road is home to an exciting assortment of edgy boutiques, stylish cafés, and hole-in-the-wall restaurants.

10 Shibuya 109 Building

MAP B6 ■ 2-29-1 Dogenzaka, Shibuya ■ www.shibuya109.jp

The cutting-edge clothes sold inside this cylindrical-shaped building are a measure of tomorrow's fashion trends.

Places to Eat

PRICE CATEGORIES
Price ranges are for dinner for one, with a drink. Lunchtime menus are usually less expensive.

¥ under ¥3,000 ¥¥ ¥3,000–¥8,000
¥¥¥ over ¥8,000

1 Fonda de la Madrugada

MAP B5 ■ Villa Bianca B1F, 2-33-12 Jingumae, Shibuya ■ 5410-6288 ■ ¥¥

This Mexican cantina offers enchiladas, stuffed chillies, and tortillas.

2 Den

MAP C5 ■ 2-3-18 Jingumae, Shibuya ■ Closed Sun ■ www.jimbochoden.com ■ ¥¥¥

The creative Japanese cuisine at Den *(see p62)* is out of this world. Order the *omakase* (chef's choice) course and see what he comes up with.

3 Sakura Tei

MAP B5 ■ 3-20-1 Jingumae, Shibuya ■ www.sakuratei.co.jp ■ ¥

This colorful place in Design Festa focuses on *okonomiyaki* – savory pancakes with a filling of meat, vegetables, and seafood.

4 Maisen

MAP S4 ■ 4-8-5 Jingumae, Shibuya ■ 050-3188-5802 ■ ¥¥

Tonkatsu (deep-fried and breaded pork cutlets) are the specialty of this main branch of a well-known chain.

5 Gyossantei

MAP A6 ■ Fontis Bldg, 2-23-12 Dogenzaka, Shibuya ■ 5489-6350 ■ Closed Sun ■ ¥¥

A cozy spot offering the regional cuisine of Miyazaki Prefecture and other Kyushu dishes.

6 Mominoki House

MAP B5 ■ 2-18-5 Jingumae, Shibuya ■ 3405-9144 ■ ¥¥

This place mostly dishes up healthy portions of vegetarian fare, although there are some departures, such as the venison and fish dishes. Only organic ingredients and ionized water are used in the food here.

7 Ghungroo

MAP S5 ■ Seinan Bldg, 5-9-6 Minamiaoyama, Minato ■ 3406-0464 ■ ¥¥

Ghungroo is a cut above many other Indian restaurants in Tokyo, a reputation gained for its delicious cuisine that is made using traditional spices and served in elegant surroundings.

8 Maruhachi

MAP B6 ■ 2-10-12 Dogenzaka, Shibuya ■ 3476-5739 ■ ¥¥

This friendly *izakaya* has an eclectic menu that covers everything from Okinawan flavors to jerk chicken, plus an extensive selection of 20 to 25 per cent *shochu* spirits.

9 Jangara Ramen

MAP Q4 ■ 1-13-21 Jingumae, Shibuya ■ 3404-5572 ■ ¥

Tonkotsu (pork bone) ramen is the best of the Kyushu-style dishes that are on the menu here.

***Tonkotsu* ramen at Jangara Ramen**

10 d47 SHOKUDO

MAP B6 ■ Shibuya Hikarie 8F, 2-21-1 Shibuya, Shibuya ■ www.hikarie8.com/en ■ ¥

The comprehensive menu at this swanky canteen features regional dishes and drinks from each of Japan's 47 prefectures, allowing you to travel the country through taste. The menu changes monthly.

See map on p100 ←

TOP 10 Shinjuku

Resembling an all-purpose city, Shinjuku is replete with large parks, train stations, shopping complexes, and department stores. Railway lines split the area into two. The windy avenues in West Shinjuku are dominated by offices, stores, and experimental skyscrapers. East Shinjuku is a legacy of the 1960s, when the area's Bohemian quarter attracted artists, writers, and political activists. Though cultural features exist on both sides, East Shinjuku appears more hedonistic, with its neon-illuminated nightspots and a sprawling red-light district.

The neon lights of Kabukicho

1 Kabukicho

MAP B3 ■ Kabukicho, Shinjuku

Kabukicho still has the touts and adult venues that earned it its reputation for being Tokyo's most notorious red-light district, but these days such venues are part of a neon-drenched hodgepodge mostly comprising legitimate bars, restaurants, live-music houses, and clubs. At night, the area comes to life.

SHINJUKU

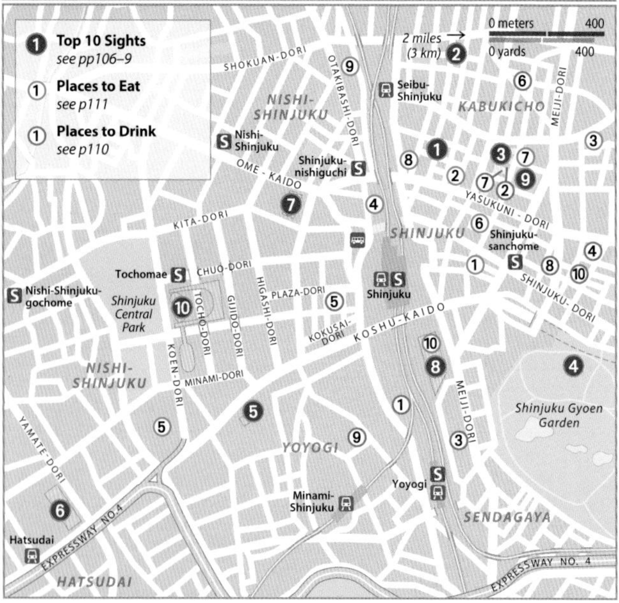

2 Yayoi Kusama Museum

MAP C3 ■ 107 Bentencho, Shinjuku ■ Open 11am–5:30pm Thu–Sun ■ Adm ■ www.yayoikusamamuseum.jp/en

Tucked away in Shinjuku's suburbs, this museum is dedicated to Japan's queen of the avant-garde, Yayoi Kusama. Founded in 2017 by Kusama herself, the museum displays major pieces from her early years to the present day, including her famous pumpkins and a version of the iconic Narcissus Garden installation. The museum hosts two exhibitions every year, plus events and lectures on contemporary art, which are highly popular, so advance bookings are essential.

3 Golden Gai

MAP B3 ■ Kabukichi 1-chome area, Shinjuku

A labyrinth of more than 200 tiny, time-warped watering holes clusters along Golden Gai's four pedestrian lanes. Dating from just after World War II, these bars are popular with local office workers, and are also patronized by writers, sumo wrestlers, and cross-dressers. Most of the establishments here charge a ¥1000 seating fee for starters.

4 Shinjuku Gyoen

MAP B4 ■ 11 Naitomachi, Shinjuku ■ 3350-0151 ■ Open mid-Mar–Sep: 9am–5:30pm Tue–Sun (to 6:30pm Jul–Aug; 4pm Oct–mid-Mar) ■ Adm ■ www.env.go.jp/garden/shinjukugyoen/english

Part of the estate of the Naito feudal clan, this large garden became an imperial retreat in 1906. Now open to the public, Shinjuku Gyoen offers Japanese, French, and English gardens, a greenhouse, and a traditional teahouse. Interestingly, tests have shown that the park is consistently two degrees or more cooler than the surrounding urban area.

Bunka Gakuen Costume Museum

5 Bunka Gakuen Costume Museum

MAP A4 ■ 3-22-7 Yoyogi, Shibuya ■ Open 10am–4:30pm Mon–Sat ■ Adm ■ www.museum.bunka.ac.jp/english

This remarkable museum is a part of Bunka Gakuen University, a fashion design school. It's historical collection, a fraction of which can be shown at a time, ranges from a Heian-era 12-layered elaborate kimono to costumes worn by Noh actors. More modern designs include the Japanese take on the Swinging Sixties. Scrolls and illustrations depict the types of clothing worn by Japanese people through the ages.

Shinjuku Gyoen

ASIAN FOOD IN SHIN-OKUBO

The diversity of modern Tokyo can be best experienced in the cosmopolitan, but down-to-earth, Shin-Okubo district. It is home to almost every conceivable Asian nationality, hence its sobriquet, "Little Asia." Apart from Chinese restaurants, Korean barbeques, and Burmese restaurants, the area also has several Thai, Indian, and Malaysian curry spots.

6 NTT InterCommunication Center

MAP A4 ■ Tokyo Opera City Tower, 4F, 3-20-2 Nishishinjuku, Shinjuku ■ Open 11am–6pm Tue–Sun ■ www.ntticc.or.jp

Part of the Tokyo Opera City office and culture complex, the center holds fascinating exhibitions that show the link between technology and creativity. Run by the telecom giant NTT, the permanent and temporary installations, video art, and interactive displays explore the connection between art, media design, and the latest techno wizardry. The excellent video library shows experimental films and video art, and features the work of cutting-edge artists, including Steina Vasulka and Nam June Paik.

NTT InterCommunication Center

Van Gogh's *Sunflowers*, Sompo Museum of Art

7 Sompo Museum of Art

MAP A3 ■ Sompo Japan Bldg, 42F, 1-26-1 Nishishinjuku, Shinjuku ■ Open 10am–6pm Tue–Sun ■ Adm ■ www.sompo-museum.org

This museum was founded in 1976 to showcase the works of Seiji Togo (1897–1978), an artist whose images, mainly of women, hover between Art Deco, Cubism, and Japanese animation figures. There are also a number of paintings by European artists such as Gauguin and Cézanne. The insurance company that owns the building made news in the 1980s "bubble economy" years when it bought Van Gogh's *Sunflowers* for an unheard-of ¥5 billion.

8 Takashimaya Times Square

MAP B4 ■ 5-24-2 Sendagaya, Shibuya ■ Open 10:30am–7:30pm daily (restaurants to 11pm) ■ www.takashimaya-global.com

A shopping haven, this 15-story department store offers something for everyone. Besides the fashion and accessory departments, restaurants, cafés, and well-stocked food basement, there is a branch of Tokyu Hands, a large and fascinating hardware store packed with diverse items related to daily living. Of special interest to foreigners is a branch of

Kinokuniya, a huge bookstore with a floor set aside for books in English and other languages.

9 Hanazono Shrine

MAP B3 ▪ 5-17-3 Shinjuku, Shinjuku ▪ 3209-5265

With orange pillars and vermillion walls, this shrine has been rebuilt several times since it was founded in the 16th century. Its presiding deity is Takeru Yamato, a legendary prince. Devotees stop by to petition the gods for luck. Rows of red and white paper lanterns illuminate the shrine's entrances at night.

The imposing Tokyo Metropolitan Government Building

10 Tokyo Metropolitan Government Building

MAP A4 ▪ 2-8-1 Nishishinjuku, Shinjuku ▪ Open 9:30am–10:30pm Mon–Fri ▪ www.metro.tokyo.lg.jp/english

The Kenzo Tange-designed Tokyo Metropolitan Government Building (Tocho) is part of a grove of sky-scrapers that have been described as everything from a mini-Manhattan to a row of grave markers. Tocho's twin 48-story towers have free obser-vation rooms, accessed via high-speed elevators. The 360-degree views from the top are superlative.

A DAY IN EAST SHINJUKU

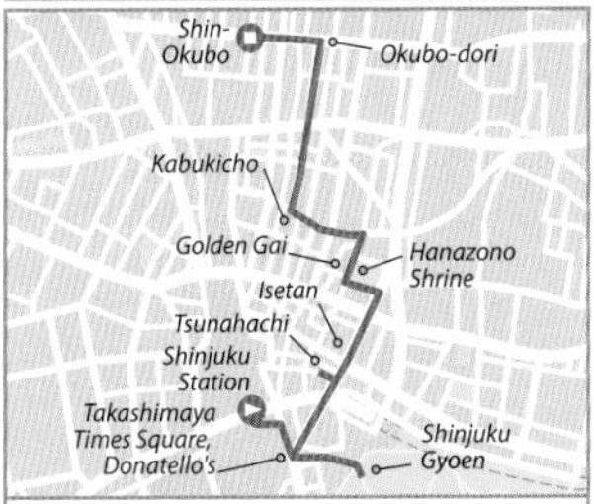

MORNING

Leaving the south exit of JR Shinjuku Station, walk down to **Shinjuku Gyoen** *(see p107)*, a spacious national garden. An entire morning can be spent here, but continue instead to **Takashimaya Times Square** *(see p108)*, a vast department store. Donatello's, on the 12th floor, serves good gelato, ice cream, and coffee. Take a short walk along Meiji-dori to the corner of Shinjuku-dori and Isetan, a department store and Tokyo institution. The sixth-floor Isetan Art Gallery showcases the latest trends in Japan's ceramic, print, and fine-art world. Walk up Shinjuka-dori, turn left and follow the road to **Tsunahachi** *(see p111)* on the right. The traditional restaurant serves tempura lunch sets at moderate prices.

AFTERNOON

Walk north until you reach the gates of **Hanazono Shrine**, whose grounds are right next to **Golden Gai** *(see p107)*, a quadrangle of bars; however, lanes will be fairly empty at this time. Walk into adjacent **Kabukicho** *(see p106)* and take almost any street north toward Okubo-dori, the main street cutting through Shin-Okubo. The district has many small temples and fox shrines, as well as Christian churches catering to a number of Korean worshipers. Have an early dinner at one of the excellent restaurants in Shin-Okubo before heading back to the bars of Golden Gai.

See map on p106

Places to Drink

1 Petit Delirium

MAP V3 ■ Shinjuku Southern Terrace, 2-2-1 Yoyogi, Shibuya ■ 6300-0807

This cozy Belgian bar offers an impressive range of bottled and draft beers, and good food.

2 Albatross G

MAP V2 ■ 2F, 5th Avenue, 1-1-7 Kabukicho, Shinjuku ■ 3203-3699 ■ Adm ■ www.alba-s.com/#/f2

The long counter, generous space, and ¥500 seating charge set this place apart from the usual run of cramped Golden Gai bars.

A bartender at Watering Hole

3 Watering Hole

MAP V3 ■ 5-26-5 Sendagaya, Shibuya ■ 6380-6115

Offering 21 beers on tap, this pleasant bar, located close to Shinjuku Gyoen garden, has the best range of craft brews in Shinjuku.

4 Aiiro Café

MAP W3 ■ 7th Tenka Bldg, 1F, 2-18-1 Shinjuku, Shinjuku ■ 6273-0740

Set in Shinjuku ni-chome, an area home to more than 500 LGBTQ+ venues, this is a highly popular, open-air café bar. It attracts a mixed, though mostly gay crowd.

5 Ben Fiddich

MAP U3 ■ 1-13-7 Nishishinjuku, Shinjuku ■ 6258-0309

Mixologist Hiroyasu Kayama's bar looks old-fashioned, but his cocktails are as creative as they come.

6 Roof Top Bar & Terrace G

MAP W2 ■ 2-14-5 Kabukicho, Shinjuku ■ www.granbellhotel.jp

The drinks menu is pretty standard, but the views at this chilled-out spot atop the Grandbell Hotel Shinjuku are out of this world.

7 Bar Plastic Model

MAP V2 ■ 1-1-10 Kabukicho, Shinjuku ■ 5273-8441 ■ Adm

A 1980s music soundtrack throbs in the background at Bar Plastic Model, one of Golden Gai's more contemporary theme bars.

8 8bitcafe

MAP W2 ■ 3-8-9 Shinjuku, Shinjuku ■ 3358-0407

Popular with gamers, this convivial spot features a menu that includes cocktails named after video game characters. There are retro game machines, so guests can play as they drink.

9 Spincoaster

MAP U3 ■ 2-26-2 Yoyogi, Shibuya ■ 6300-9211

Located halfway between Shinjuku and Yoyogi stations, this hip bar with a state-of-the-art sound system plays an eclectic stream of music on vinyl.

10 Bar Gold Finger

MAP W3 ■ 2-12-11 Shinjuku, Shinjuku ■ 6383-4649

A bar popular with the LGBTQ+ community in Shinjuku ni-chome, Tokyo's famous gay district. Saturday nights are for women only.

Places to Eat

PRICE CATEGORIES
Price ranges are for dinner for one, with a drink. Lunchtime menus are usually less expensive.

¥ under ¥3,000 ¥¥ ¥3,000–¥8,000
¥¥¥ over ¥8,000

1 Tsunahachi

MAP V2 ■ 3-31-8 Shinjuku, Shinjuku ■ 3352-1012 ■ ¥¥

Huge portions of deep-fried tempura served in a prewar building offer good value. English menu available.

2 Tokaien

MAP V2 ■ 1-6-3 Kabukicho, Shinjuku ■ 3200-2934 ■ ¥¥

Over nine floors, Tokaien serves superb *yakiniku* (Korean-style barbecue). The sixth floor offers an all-you-can-eat menu.

3 Sansar

MAP W2 ■ 6-13-8 Shinjuku, Shinjuku ■ 3354-8553 ■ ¥¥

Friendly Nepali staff serve up a standard Indian repertoire, plus some delicious Nepalese specialties.

4 Omoide-Yokocho

MAP V2 ■ Nishishinjuku 1-chome area, Shinjuku ■ ¥¥

This atmospheric warren of lanes is full of smoky *yakitori* chicken stalls, noodle stores, and bars.

Food stalls in Omoide-Yokocho

New York Grill's chic dining room

5 New York Grill

MAP T3 ■ Park Hyatt Hotel, 52F, 3-7-12 Nishishinjuku, Shinjuku ■ 5323-3458 ■ ¥¥¥

One of the leading grill restaurants in Tokyo, this restaurant serves a great range of meat and seafood options.

6 Tavolo di Fiori

MAP V2 ■ 3-16-13 Shinjuku, Shinjuku ■ 3354-3790 ■ ¥¥

A traditional trattoria, with delicious Tuscan fare served by genial staff.

7 Youichi

MAP W2 ■ 2-8-12 Kabukicho, Shinjuku ■ 6457-6929 ■ ¥¥

This venue specializes in *jingisukan* (aka Genghis Khan) – a dish with lamb and vegetables grilled over a skillet.

8 Ban Thai

MAP V2 ■ Dai-ichi Metro Bldg, 3F, 1-23-14 Kabukicho, Shinjuku ■ 3207-0068 ■ ¥¥

This popular place was one of Tokyo's first Thai restaurants.

9 Menya Musashi

MAP U3 ■ K1 Bldg, 1F, 7-2-6 Nishishinjuku, Shinjuku ■ www.menya634.co.jp ■ ¥

It is widely regarded as among the best ramen shops in Tokyo.

10 Imahan

MAP Q2 ■ Times Square Bldg, 14F, 5-24-2 Sendagaya, Shibuya ■ 5361-1871 ■ ¥¥

Expect generous portions at this food place known for *sukiyaki* (sliced meat with vegetables) and *shabu-shabu*.

See map on p106

TOP 10 Farther Afield

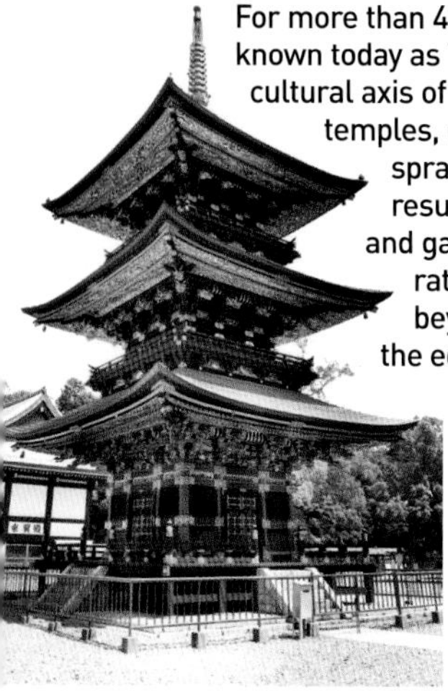

For more than 400 years, all roads have led to the city known today as Tokyo, the political, commercial, and cultural axis of Japan. Significant ports, trading posts, temples, mausoleums, and leisure resorts sprang up along these highways. As a result, ideas about architecture, religion, and gardening coursed into the city. A first-rate train service makes it easy to explore beyond the megalopolis, and for sights at the edges of the city, Tokyo's subway system is unmatched. Sumptuous tombs in Nikko, the ancient city of Kamakura, and the Edo-era Kawagoe invoke the past. Alternatively, hiking at Mount Fuji or Mount Takao is very rewarding, as is exploring Yokohama, Japan's second-largest city.

Naritasan Shinsho-ji Temple

FARTHER AFIELD

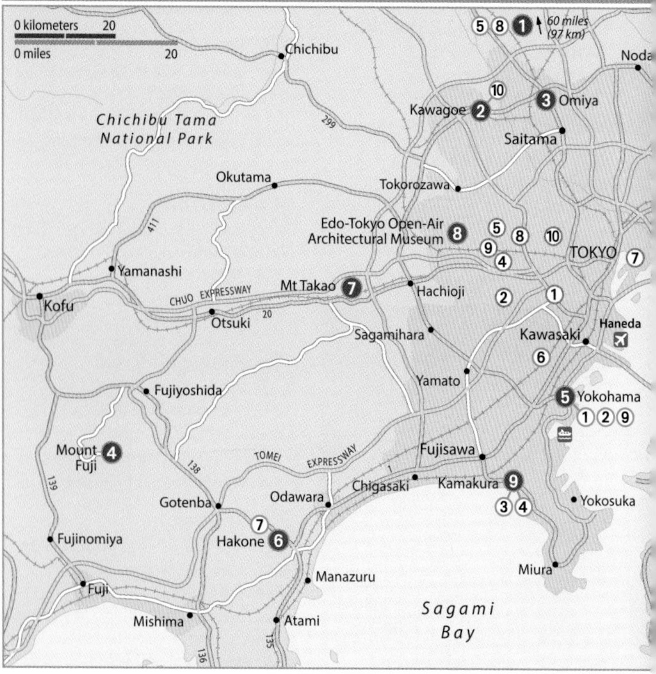

Detail of wood carvings at Toshogu Shrine, Nikko

1 Nikko

MAP B1 ■ Nikko, Tochigi Prefecture ■ Tobu Line from Asakusa ■ Toshogu Shrine ■ Open 9am–5pm daily (to 4pm Nov–Mar) ■ Adm

Nikko's opulent temples, religious art, sacred storehouses, and tombs are more Rococo than Zen. Chosen in 1617 as the burial site of the shogun Ieyasu, Toshogu Shrine is a complex of buildings and mausoleums. It is best accessed by the tree-lined avenue leading to Rinno-ji Temple, with its thousand-armed Kannon statue and five-storied pagoda. The Yomei-mon gate to Toshogu Shrine is lavishly painted and carved. Ieyasu's tomb lies a little higher up a forest path.

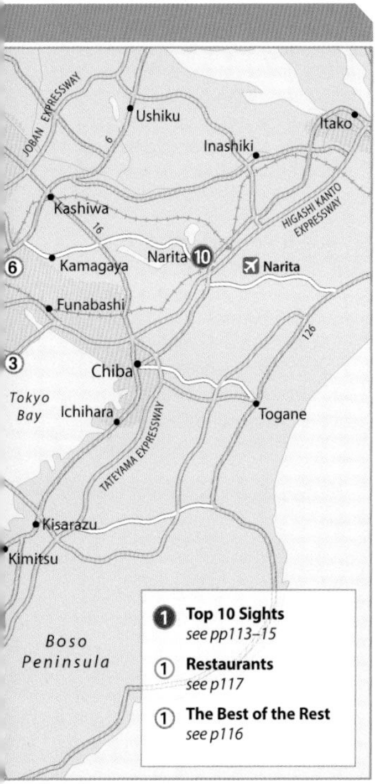

2 Kawagoe

MAP B1 ■ Kawagoe, Saitama Prefecture ■ Tobu Tojo Line from Ikebukuro

Known as "Little Edo," Kawagoe once supplied goods for Edo. Today, the town's main draw is its high street, Ichiban-gai. Many of its traditional warehouses have been converted into stores, galleries, and museums. Yamawa, a ceramic store inside one of the buildings, is a fine example of the architecture of these fireproof structures. Toki no Kane, a wooden bell tower off the main street, has become a symbol of the town.

3 Railway Museum, Omiya

MAP B1 ■ JR lines from Ueno ■ Open 10am–5pm Wed–Mon ■ Adm ■ www.railway-museum.jp/e

This interactive museum *(see p54)* is devoted to the history of Japan's railways. There are 30-odd previously used train engines and carriages on display, and you can play at driving a *shinkansen* (bullet train).

Engines on display, Railway Museum

4 Mount Fuji and Kawaguchi-ko

MAP A2 ■ Express Keio bus from Shinjuku Station

Sacred Fuji-san, Japan's highest peak, is a beautiful sight close up, particularly in good weather, and the officially active volcano can be seen from the shores of the lakes to its north. The best lake to stay near is Kawaguchi-ko, which has a good range of accommodations and a cable car to the Fuji Viewing Platform.

View of Mount Fuji over a lake

5 Yokohama

MAP B2 ■ Yokohama ■ JR Tokaido Line from Tokyo; Tokyu Toyoko and Minato Mirai subway from Shibuya

A crucial Meiji-era foreign settlement and port, Yokohama includes the Minato Mirai complex, with an art museum, amusement park, stores, and Japan's second-tallest building – Landmark Tower. Moored nearby is a fine old clipper, the *Nippon Maru*. The area offers visitors restaurants and shopping streets of Chinatown, silk and doll museums, old customs buildings, and a lovely Japanese garden, Sankei-en.

6 Hakone

MAP A2 ■ Odakyu express bus from Shinjuku; Odakyu Line from Shinjuku

The pleasant switchback route up the slopes on the Hakone Tozan Railway starts at Hakone-Yumato, a hot-spring town. Alight at Miyanoshita, stopping for tea at the Fujiya Hotel *(see p133)*. Farther up, the Hakone Open-Air Museum features sculpture by the likes of Rodin and Henry Moore. Gora is the terminus; take the funicular and cable car to the shore of Lake Ashi, stopping off on the way at Owakudani volcanic valley.

EAST MEETS WEST

On July 8, 1853, Commodore Perry, hoping to open Japan to foreign trade and diplomacy, sailed "black ships" into Edo Bay *(see p38)*. The ritual exchange of gifts that ensued – a bronze temple bell and teapot on the Japanese side, a telegraph machine and daguerreotype camera from the visitors – showed how much progress had bypassed Japan.

7 Mount Takao

MAP B2 ■ Keio Line from Shinjuku Station ■ www.takaosan-onsen.jp/english

Far easier than climbing Mount Fuji, this Quasi-National park has hiking trails as well as a cable car and chair lifts. Near the summit is the Yakuo-in, an 8th-century temple, which hosts a fire festival on the second Sunday in March. The train station, designed by Kengo Kuma, has an open-air bath to relax in before or after your climb.

8 Edo-Tokyo Open Air Architectural Museum

MAP B1 ■ 3-7-1 Sakuracho, Koganai ■ Musashi Koganei, Chuo Line ■ Open Apr–Sep: 9:30am–5:30pm Tue–Sat; Oct–Mar: 9:30am–4:30pm Tue–Sun ■ Adm ■ www.tatemonoen.jp

Buildings representative of Tokyo during the Edo, Meiji, and later

The fascinating Edo-Tokyo Open Air Architectural Museum

periods have been collected and reassembled in this open-air architectural museum, a branch of the Edo-Tokyo Museum in Ryogoku. The museum's farmhouses, villas, public buildings, and bathhouse are set in the middle of Koganei Park.

Daibutsu Buddha, Kamakura

9 Kamakura

MAP B2 ■ JR Yokosuka line from Tokyo, Shimbashi, Shinagawa

The shogun's capital from 1192 to 1333, this seaside town has ancient shrines, gardens, and the Daibutsu Buddha statue. Of its two stations, Kita-Kamakura is close to Engaku-ji Temple and the gardens of Meigetsu-in Temple. Kamakura Station is near the local craft and food stores along Wakamiya-oji and Komachi streets, and Tsurugaoka Hachiman-gu Shrine.

10 Naritasan Shinsho-ji Temple

MAP B1 ■ JR or Keisei trains from Ueno ■ www.naritasan.or.jp/english

Established in 940, this beautifully decorated and atmospheric Buddhist temple is set in extensive grounds. Close to Narita Airport, this large complex is a popular pilgrimage location, approached by an appealing shopping street lined with traditional craft stores and restaurants specializing in *unagi* (eel).

TWO DAYS IN KAMAKURA

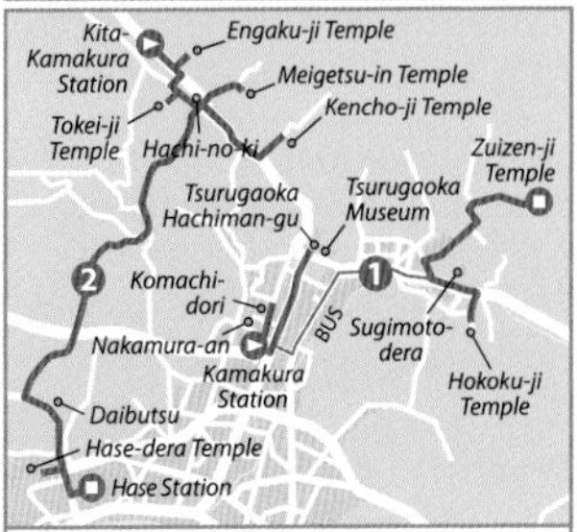

DAY 1

Exiting at **Kamakura** Station, take Komachi-dori, a street with cafés and specialist stores. Return to the station area and take Wakamiya-oji, a street selling local products. At the end of the road, Tsurugaoka Hachiman-gu, **Kamakura's** premier shrine, is dedicated to the god of war. Back at the entrance, turn left for the Tsurugaoka Museum. Stop for tasty noodles at Nakamura-an, along a narrow lane between Wakamiya-oji and Komachi-dori. Take a bus from the No. 5 stop outside the station to Sugimoto-dera, the area's oldest temple. Across the road, Hokoku-ji Temple is perfect for tea at the pavilion. A short walk away, Zuizen-ji is a Zen temple with a 14th-century garden.

DAY 2

Get off at Kita-Kamakura Station and stroll to Engaku-ji Temple. Walk over the railroad crossing opposite for Tokei-ji Temple. Recross the tracks and walk south to Meigetsu-in Temple. Return to the road and stroll south toward the wooden gates of Kencho-ji Temple. Stop at Hachi-no-ki Honten next door for *shojin ryori* (Buddhist vegetarian cuisine). Retrace your steps until you see a hiking path sign. Turn left for the Daibutsu, the Great Buddha statue. Follow the road to Hase-dera temple, with a view of the bay and town. Take the Enoden Line for Kamakura Station at **Hase Station** nearby.

See map on p112–13

The Best of the Rest

1 Gotoh Art Museum

MAP C2 ■ 3-9-25 Kaminoge, Setagaya ■ Open 10am–5pm Tue–Sun ■ Adm ■ www.gotoh-museum.or.jp

A private collection of Buddhist calligraphy, painting, and rare scrolls.

2 Nihon Minka-en

MAP B2 ■ 7-1-1 Masugata, Kawasaki ■ Open Mar–Oct: 9:30am–5pm; Nov–Feb: 9:30am–4:30pm ■ Adm ■ www.nihonminkaen.jp

Traditional farmhouses, merchant homes, tools, and domestic utensils make up this open-air folk museum.

3 Tokyo Disney Resort®

MAP B2 ■ 1-1 Maihama, Urayasu, Chiba Prefecture ■ Opening times vary, check website ■ Adm ■ www.tokyodisneyresort.jp

Kids will love the popular attractions at Disneyland® and DisneySea®.

4 Jindaiji Temple

MAP A1 ■ 5-15-1 Jindaijimoto-machi, Chofu ■ www.jindaiji.or.jp/en

Set in quiet natural surrounds that feel far removed from Tokyo, Jindaiji is home to a priceless 7th-century bronze statue of Buddha. The neighboring Jindai Botanical Gardens, with around 5,000 rose varieties, are divine.

5 Inokashira Park

MAP B2 ■ 1-18-31 Gotenyama, Musashino

A popular cherry blossom-viewing venue in early April. On weekends, musicians, market stalls, and street artists take over its paths.

6 Shibamata

MAP B1

Location of the film series *Otoko wa Tsurai Yo* (It's Tough Being a Man), this eastern Tokyo neighborhood has retro charm. Its main shopping street leads to Taishakuten Temple.

7 Museum of Contemporary Art (MOT)

MAP C2 ■ 4-1-1 Miyoshi, Koto ■ 5633-5860 ■ Open 10am–6pm Tue–Sun ■ Adm ■ www.mot-art-museum.jp/en

Next to Kiba Park, this large, modern museum displays post-1945 art from Japan and overseas.

8 Suginami Animation Museum

MAP B1 ■ 3-29-5 Kamiogi, Suginami ■ 3396-1510 ■ Open 10am–6pm Tue–Sun ■ www.sam.or.jp

Kids and Japanese animation fans will appreciate this free museum with displays devoted to the history of anime and some of its most beloved characters.

9 Ghibli Museum

MAP B1 ■ 1-1-83 Shimorenjaku, Mitaka ■ Open 10am–6pm Wed–Mon ■ Adm (advance ticket only) ■ www.ghibli-museum.jp

Attracts admirers of the work of animator Hayao Miyazaki.

10 Nakano

MAP C1

Three stops west on the Chuo Line from Shinjuku, Nakano is known for its 1960s shopping strip with stores specializing in anime and manga.

Boating at Inokashira Park

Restaurants

PRICE CATEGORIES
Price ranges are for dinner for one, with a drink. Lunchtime menus are usually less expensive.

¥ under ¥3,000 ¥¥ ¥3,000–¥8,000
¥¥¥ over ¥8,000

1 Heichinro Yokohama Honten

MAP B2 ■ 149 Yamashitacho, Naka, Yokohama ■ 045-681-3001 ■ ¥¥

Set amidst Yokohama's Chinatown district, this oldest operating Chinese restaurant offers delectable dim sums, and impeccable service.

2 Mutekiro

MAP B2 ■ 2-96 Motomachi, Naka, Yokohama ■ 045-681-2926 ■ Opening times vary, call ahead ■ ¥¥¥

Exquisite French food, with a little French pomp thrown in, is the main draw of this place. Set in Yokohama's fashionable Motomachi district, this is a great spot for a romantic meal.

3 Matsubara-an

MAP B2 ■ 4-10-3 Yuigahama, Kamakura ■ 0467-61-3838 ■ ¥¥

Fine soba noodles and other dishes are served in a lovely wooden house in a quiet part of Kamakura. In good weather, there's seating in its garden.

4 Gentoan

MAP B2 ■ 823 Yamanouchi, Kamakura ■ Closed Mon ■ www.gentouan.jp/en ■ ¥¥¥

Beyond Gentoan's attractive stone entryway await *kaiseki ryori* dishes that are so perfectly presented it seems a crime to devour them.

5 Meguri

MAP B1 ■ 909-1 Nakahatsuishi-machi, Nikko ■ 0288-25-3122 ■ Closed Thu ■ ¥

Arrive at opening time to be sure of scoring one of the limited number of delicious vegetarian lunches served at this rustic café located on Nikko's main road.

6 Shin-Yokohama Ramen Museum

MAP B2 ■ 2-14-21 Shin-Yokohama, Kohoku ■ 045-471-0503 ■ ¥

The history of Japanese noodles is upstaged by the basement restaurant selling Japan's favorite ramen from Hokkaido to Kyushu.

Restaurant at the Fujiya Hotel

7 Fujiya Hotel

MAP A2 ■ 359 Miyanoshita, Hakone ■ www.fujiyahotel.jp ■ ¥¥¥

Waitstaff in old-fashioned aprons serve delicious Western dishes in a setting that has changed little since the hotel opened in 1878.

8 Gyoshintei

MAP B1 ■ 2339-1 Sannai, Nikko ■ www.meiji-yakata.com/en/gyoshin ■ ¥¥

Buddhist vegetarian and *kaiseki-ryori* dishes come with views of moss and pine trees in a park-like setting.

9 Bashamichi Taproom

MAP B2 ■ 5-63-1 Sumiyoshicho, Naka, Yokohama ■ www.bairdbeer.com/taprooms/bashamichi ■ ¥¥

An American-style barbecue, with smoked meats slow-cooked to perfection over a cherrywood fire.

10 Ichinoya

MAP B2 ■ 1-18-10 Matsuecho, Kawagoe ■ 049-222-0354 ■ ¥¥

Traditional eel dishes, a Kawagoe specialty, are served here on a bed of rice along with miso soup and pickles.

See map on p112–13

Streetsmart

A colorful street in the Kabukicho district, Shinjuku

Getting Around **120**

Practical Information **124**

Places to Stay **128**

General Index **134**

Acknowledgments **139**

Phrase Book **141**

Getting Around

Arriving by Air

Many airlines, including the national airline JAL (Japan Airlines) and ANA (All Nippon Airways), fly into **Narita International Airport**, (41 miles) 66 km east of central Tokyo, from overseas. **Haneda Airport**, (12 miles) 20 km south of Tokyo, also has a growing number of international connections.

The fastest way into Tokyo from Narita is on the **Keisei Skyliner**, which takes 41 minutes to reach Ueno, where you can connect with the JR Yamanote Line or subways. **Japan Railways (JR)** also runs frequent Narita Express (N'EX) services to Tokyo (53 minutes). Visitors can buy a discount return N'EX ticket valid for 14 days.

Haneda Airport is connected to the city center by both the Tokyo Monorail (15 minutes to Hamamatsucho) and the **Keikyu** train line (13 minutes to Shinagawa).

The **Airport Limousine Bus** runs between Narita and Haneda airports to major Tokyo train stations and hotels.

A taxi from Narita to central Tokyo will cost you around ¥25,000 while one from Haneda will be around ¥7,000.

Train Travel

Tokyo's railroad system is the most extensive and busiest in the world, but it is also extremely clean, efficient, safe, and famously punctual. The system is very well organized, with color-coded maps, directional arrows, and bilingual signs. Trains run from 5am to just after midnight daily. Avoid rush hour (8–9am and 6–8pm) if possible, especially if you are carrying luggage or traveling with small kids.

Train Lines

There are several private railroad companies running in Tokyo, as well as an excellent subway system run by the Tokyo Metro and Toei Subway companies *(see p122)*. Despite the multitude of operators, transferring between lines is rarely troublesome due to good signage and a digitized ticketing system. Trains running on the same lines are usually divided into *tokkyu* ("limited express"), kyuko ("express"), *kaisoku* ("rapid"), and *futsu* ("local"), so it is important to check the type of train before boarding as express trains skip many smaller local stations.

For those wanting to travel around the country, Tokyo Station is the major terminus for the *shinkansen*, although those traveling on the Tokaido Line to western destinations, including Kyoto and Hiroshima, can also board the bullet train at Shinagawa Station. Tickets and reservations for the bullet train can be bought at most JR stations in Tokyo. Seat reservations, which are charged at a small extra fee, are recommended for long-distance trips.

Passes

The **Japan Rail Pass** (JR Pass) is recommended for those planning to travel extensively throughout Japan, but a number of JR regional rail passes are also available that cover specific areas closer to Tokyo. For those not traveling too far from the capital, there is the **JR TOKYO Wide Pass** which covers popular sites in the region, including Lake Kawaguchi and Nikko.

Long-Distance Bus Travel

The efficiency and extent of the rail network mean that few visitors to Tokyo use long-distance coaches to travel to and from the city, but Japan's highway bus network is comprehensive, and for those without a JR Pass, a bus is a much cheaper option than the bullet train.

Multiple companies run long-distance services from the capital. Coaches depart from many locations around the city – usually near major train stations – but the epicenter of bus travel in Tokyo is the modern, multi-story **Shinjuku Expressway Bus Terminal**. This is located across the road from Shinjuku Station's South Exit.

Tokyo Station is the other major junction for buses coming to and from the city. The **Tokyo Expressway Bus Terminal** is situated on the east side of the station.

Public Transportation

The Tokyo Metropolitan Bureau of Transportation, or **Toei**, is Tokyo's main public transportation authority. Safety and hygiene measures, timetables, ticket information, transport maps, and more can be obtained on its website, at tourist information centers, and stations.

Tickets

Basic fare tickets for short distances are bought from ticket machines at stations, and virtually all of these will have an English-translation button and accept credit and debit cards. Most stations have maps in English, indicating the fares to different destinations. If in doubt about the cost of a trip, simply buy a cheap ticket and pay any excess at the destination using the fare adjustment machine near the exit barrier. This machine will supply you with a new ticket. If there is no such machine, station staff will work out the additional charge; you will not be penalized for having the wrong-value ticket.

In Tokyo there are a wide variety of single or multi-day passes available for the different transport operators, but they are not usually worth the inconvenience of being limited to certain lines. The **Tokyo 1-Day Ticket** (known as "Free Kippu" in Japanese) is probably the most flexible pass option, as it allows 24 hours of unlimited travel within Tokyo's 23 wards on most of the JR, subway, bus, and streetcar lines (excluding all private railroad lines). This pass can be purchased at any JR station for ¥1,600 (children ¥800).

For those planning on making use of Tokyo's extensive subway system, it is worth considering a **Chika Toku** pass, which allows unlimited subway travel for either 24, 48 or 72 hours, and can also be used to obtain various discounts at over 250 attractions, restaurants, and shops.

Most travelers opt to buy either a **Suica**, or **Pasmo** IC card. These convenient and flexible interoperable smart cards can be used on virtually all forms of public transportation in Tokyo and surrounding areas. Suica cards can be purchased at JR train stations, either over the counter or from vending machines. Pasmo cards can be bought at stations on the subway system or at one of Tokyo's numerous private railroad line stations. There is no discernible difference between the two types of cards, which can be used interchangeably on the network and both cost ¥1,000. This price includes a ¥500 deposit which is refunded when the card is returned, along with any unused funds – although with Suica a commission fee of ¥220 is also deducted from the remaining balance. Both cards can also be used for making purchases at an increasing number of shops, including convenience stores, vending machines and station lockers – just look for a card reader with the Suica or Pasmo mark.

DIRECTORY

ARRIVING BY AIR

Airport Limousine Bus
W webservice.limousinebus.co.jp/web/en

Haneda Airport
W tokyo-haneda.com/en

Japan Railways (JR)
W jreast.co.jp/multi/en

Keikyu Trains
W haneda-tokyo-access.com

Keisei Skyliner
W keisei.co.jp

Narita International Airport
W narita-airport.jp/en

PASSES

Japan Rail Pass
W japanrailpass.net

JR TOKYO Wide Pass
W jreast.co.jp/multi/en

LONG-DISTANCE BUS TRAVEL

Shinjuku Expressway Bus Terminal
W shinjuku-busterminal.co.jp

Tokyo Expressway Bus Terminal
W jrbuskanto.co.jp/bus_stop/tokyo.html

PUBLIC TRANSPORTATION

Toei
W kotsu.metro.tokyo.jp

TICKETS

Chika Toku
W chikatoku.enjoytokyo.jp

Pasmo
W pasmo.co.jp

Suica
W jreast.co.jp/multi/en

Tokyo 1-Day Ticket
W jreast.co.jp/multi/en

Subway

Tokyo's subway network is extensive and consists of the **Tokyo Metro** (nine lines) and Toei Subway (four lines) systems. Tokyo Metro and Toei Subway have different symbols (a white "M" on a blue background and a green fan-shaped symbol respectively), but they share the same subway sign (a blue train on its track), which is usually prominent at the street-level entrance to the subway. Besides being color-coded, each subway line is designated a letter (G for the Ginza Line, for example), and each station is assigned a number. Hence, Shibuya, the western terminal of the Ginza Line, is G-01.

Color-coded subway maps in English are available at all major train and metro stations, many hotels, and tourist information centers.

Local Buses

Several bus companies connect many parts of Tokyo. This method of travel is particularly good for local hot spots that may not be on the main tourist paths, and therefore not easily reached by subway or train – however, the lack of English signage can pose more of a difficulty.

Bus stands *(basu noriba)* are usually located in front of major train stations. Buses in central Tokyo have a flat-fare system and charge ¥210 (¥110 for children). Unlike in many other parts of Japan, you board the bus by the front door, place your fare in the box beside the driver or touch your prepaid Suica or Pasmo card on the sensor, and exit from the door in the middle of the bus.

Trams

The city's last two remaining tramlines hark back to an older, more leisurely era and can be a pleasant respite from the city's crowded trains. The Arakawa Line trundles through the backstreets of northern Tokyo. The stations at either end have subway connections, and the tram can also be boarded at Otsuka Station, where it crosses the JR Yamanote Line. In the west of the city, the Setagaya Line links Sangenjaya Station (for the Denentoshi Line) and Shimotakaido Station (Keio Line).

Taxis

Taxis come in various colors, but all have a "Taxi" sign on the roof. A red sign to the left of the driver indicates that the taxi is free. You can flag a taxi on the street or look for a stand: they are frequently located near main stations, hotels, and department stores.

The starting rate for taxis in Tokyo is ¥410 for the first 0.5 miles (1 km), which increases by ¥80 every 260 yds (237 m). Fares are around 20 per cent higher at night between 10pm and 5am and also increase in standing traffic. Tipping is not required.

Drivers operate taxi doors from inside so you do not need to bother opening and closing them. Few taxi drivers speak much English, so it is best to carry a map or an address of your destination in Japanese if hailing a cab in the street. Potential communication difficulties can be avoided by ordering or reserving a taxi in advance by phone or online, as many Tokyo taxi companies do have English websites, apps, and bilingual call centers – although you will normally be charged an additional reservation fee.

Ride-share services such as Uber have a very small imprint in Tokyo and are almost nonexistent outside the capital due to Japan's strict legal restrictions on taxi services. As a cab hailing service, **JapanTaxi**'s app is more useful as it is linked to most of the city's major taxi companies.

Driving

With roads often clogged with traffic, trains are the best way of exploring Tokyo and the surrounding area. Even when traveling farther afield, the railway is a better option than driving, as Japan's rail system leads the world in terms of efficiency, safety, and comfort.

Car Rental

Renting a car in Tokyo is not recommended; few roads are signposted in English, and although rental cars usually feature sat nav systems, the on-screen text is in Japanese. If you wish to explore Japan by car, head out of Tokyo by train and rent a vehicle in a smaller town. The **Japan Automobile Federation** (JAF) offers details about car rental companies.

Cycling

Cycling is an extremely popular way of getting around Tokyo, and it can often be the fastest way of traveling for distances of up to around 6 miles (10 km). Most city streets have no cycle or footpaths, so cars, bikes, and pedestrians are accustomed to sharing the same space. Even sidewalks alongside larger roads are frequently used by local cyclists, despite the fact that it is technically illegal to do so.

There are bicycle-rental companies in many big tourist areas. However, a high-tech and less tiring alternative to renting your own bicycle is the **Bike Share Service** program, which operates in 13 of the city's central wards. There are more than 900 ports where you can find these distinctive red and black E-bikes with electric-assist pedaling. Customers are free to pick up and drop off the bike at a location of their convenience. The bikes are smart-locked and have a key pad/IC card reader at the back, to activate them. Although you must register as a member in advance, this can be done easily on the website. One-day rates are available for tourists.

Walking

Wandering around Tokyo is a great way to get to know the city. As you explore on two feet, you can absorb the streetlife, take in the architectural details, and peek into any café, shop or bar that catches your interest. The districts of Ueno, Harajuku, and Shibuya are particularly pedestrian-friendly.

Water Bus

Traveling by water bus *(suijo basu)* allows you to see parts of the city usually only glimpsed through the window of a train. The most popular routes are operated by **Tokyo Cruise** and travel down the Sumida River – one of the city's most famous waterways – and around the waterfront areas of Tokyo Bay's man-made islands. All services depart from Hinode Pier, close to Hinode Station (Yurikamome Line) and a 10-minute walk from Hamamatsucho JR Station (Yamanote Line). Popular sightseeing spots can be accessed en route, including the historical district of Asakusa, the Hamarikyu Gardens, the Toyosu Fish Market and Odaiba. Boats run approximately every half-hour.

Finding an Address

Only the main thoroughfares in Tokyo tend to have street names. In an address – for example, "2-3-4 Otemachi" – the first number refers to the chome, or main block. The second number indicates a smaller block of buildings within the chome. The last is the number of a yet smaller block of buildings. The numbering system is quite complex, and it can be hard to find lesser-known sights. Officers at police boxes are used to helping people find their destinations.

Travel Etiquette

Etiquette is an important part of Japanese culture, so it may be unsurprising that there are certain things to bear in mind while traveling. When waiting for a train or bus, line up neatly, letting other people off the train first. When you're on board, hold your backpack or luggage in front of you to make space for others.Talking loudly, especially on a cell phone, is considered disrespectful toward other passengers and eating and drinking are deemed bad manners, except over long distances. When it's time to get off a crowded train, gently push through and call out *"Orimasu"* ("I'm getting off") so people know to make way.

DIRECTORY

SUBWAY

Tokyo Metro
W tokyometro.jp/en

TAXIS

JapanTaxi
W japantaxi.jp

CAR RENTAL

Japan Automobile Federation (JAF)
W english.jaf.or.jp

CYCLING

Bike Share Service
W docomo-cycle.jp

WATER BUS

Tokyo Cruise
W suijobus.co.jp/en

Practical Information

Passports and Visas

For entry requirements, including visas, consult your nearest Japanese embassy or check the **Japan Ministry of Foreign Affairs** website. EU nationals and citizens of the UK, US, Canada, Australia, New Zealand, and many other countries, do not need a visa for stays of up to three months. Citizens of some countries may extend this stay by another 90 days at immigration offices in Japan (at least 10 days before the expiration date).

Government Advice

Now more than ever, it is important to consult both your and the Japanese government's advice before travelling. The **UK Foreign and Commonwealth Office**, the **US State Department**, the **Australian Department of Foreign Affairs and Trade**, and the **Tokyo Metropolitan Government** offer the latest information on security, health, and local regulations.

Each year, Japan experiences over 1,000 earthquakes. The government has issued a useful **Disaster Preparedness Manual** with safety guidelines in the event of strong tremors.

Customs Information

You can find information on the laws relating to goods and currency taken in or out of Japan on the **Customs and Tariff Bureau**'s website.

Insurance

We recommend that you take out a comprehensive insurance policy covering theft, loss of belongings, medical care, cancellations and delays, and read the small print carefully. As a visitor, you will be expected to pay the full amount for any health treatments. Charges for consultations and drugs are high. Be sure to carry proof of health insurance.

Health

Japan has a world-class health system, but medical expenses can be extremely high. It is therefore important to arrange comprehensive medical insurance before travelling. If you are sick while in Japan, consult a doctor at a local clinic; for minor problems, see a pharmacist. For medical services in Tokyo, see **Himawari**, which is run by the Tokyo Metropolitan Government or contact the **Tokyo Foreign Residents Advisory Service**.

Tokyo has a surfeit of well-stocked pharmacies, although staff may not speak English. The **American Pharmacy** in the basement of the Marunouchi Building has English-speaking staff.

No inoculations are needed for Japan and the tap water is drinkable.

Smoking, Alcohol, and Drugs

In all central Tokyo wards, smoking on the street is banned (punishable by on-the-spot fines), except in specially designated areas. Smoking is also banned at stations and hospitals, as well as on buses and trains (except for some long-distance trains such as the *shinkansen*, which have smoking rooms between some carriages). However, smoking is still permitted in some bars and restaurants, which may have a smoking section.

Japan has a strict limit of 0.03 per cent BAC (blood alcohol content) for drivers. If a driver exceeds this limit, they will face a heavy fine and up to five years in prison.

There is a zero-tolerance policy toward the possession of even small amounts of narcotics. The punishment is a jail sentence and heavy fine.

ID

You must carry your passport or residence card with you at all times. A photocopy of your passport photo page (and visa if applicable) should suffice.

Personal Security

Tokyo is a relatively safe city to visit. Thefts and muggings are rare, but there are sporadic incidents of bag-snatching and pick-pocketing in crowded areas. It is generally safe to walk around at night, but extra care should be taken in the Roppongi and Kabukicho entertainment districts. If you have anything stolen, report the crime within 24 hours to the nearest police station and take ID with you. Contact your embassy if you have your passport stolen, or in the event of a serious crime or accident.

If you have problems making yourself understood to the **Ambulance**, **Fire**, and **Police** emergency services, contact **Himawari**.

As a rule, Tokyoites are very accepting of all people, regardless of their race, gender, or sexuality, but the city is not as multicultural as other capitals, and staring is commonplace.

Homosexuality was criminalized in Japan in 1872, but the law was repealed seven years later. Despite this historic acceptance, same-sex marriages are still not legally recognized.

LGBTQ+ travelers are unlikely to encounter any problems in Japan. Public displays of affection between both straight and same-sex couples are frowned upon by some Japanese people, but less so in Tokyo. **Utopia Asia** is a comprehensive guide to Japan's LGBTQ+ scene.

Travelers with Specific Requirements

Tokyo is not the easiest city for travelers with specific requirements to negotiate. People in wheelchairs occasionally have issues at small subway stations that don't have elevators, and at pedestrian over- and underpasses, though all new buildings and developments must have ramps installed following the 2008 law requiring barrier-free access.

The visually impaired are well provided for in Tokyo. Lines of yellow raised dots on the ground guide the visually impaired, and traffic lights have audible signals for crossing. Trains have special seats, and many ticket machines have Braille plates.

Accessible Tokyo, **Accessible Japan**, **Japan Accessible Tourism Center**, and **Japanese Red Cross Language Service Volunteers** provide information about disabled access and facilities in the capital, as well as the surrounding area, including the nearby cities of Yokohama and Kamakura.

DIRECTORY

PASSPORTS AND VISAS

Japan Ministry of Foreign Affairs
W mofa.go.jp

GOVERNMENT ADVICE

Australia Department of Foreign Affairs and Trade
W smartraveller.gov.au

Disaster Preparedness Manual
W metro.tokyo.jp/english/guide/bosai/index.html

Tokyo Metropolitan Government
W metro.tokyo.lg.jp/english/index.html

UK Foreign and Commonwealth Office
W gov.uk/foreign-travel-advice

US Department of State
W travel.state.gov

CUSTOMS INFORMATION

Customs and Tariff Bureau
W customs.go.jp/english/index.htm

HEALTH

American Pharmacy
T 5220-7716

Himawari
W himawari.metro.tokyo.jp

Tokyo Foreign Residents Advisory Service
W metro.tokyo.lg.jp/english/guide/guide01.html

PERSONAL SECURITY

Ambulance and Fire
T 119

Himawari
W himawari.metro.tokyo.jp

Police
T 110

Utopia Asia
W utopia-asia.com

TRAVELERS WITH SPECIFIC REQUIREMENTS

Accessible Japan
W accessible-japan.com

Accessible Tokyo
W accessible.jp.org

Japan Accessible Tourism Center
W japan-accessible.com

Japanese Red Cross Language Service Volunteers
W tok-lanserv.jp/eng

Time Zone

Tokyo operates on Japan Standard Time (JST), which is 9 hours ahead of Greenwich Mean Time (GMT) and 14 hours ahead of Eastern Standard Time (EST). There is no daylight-savings time.

Money

The yen (¥) is the official currency of Japan. Japan has traditionally had a cash-based economy. The move to contactless is accelerating but it's still wise to carry around some cash at all times.

Cards can be used at major stations to buy JR train tickets and are accepted by most taxis.

Tipping is not part of the culture in Japan. Attempts to do so could lead to confusion, with servers doing their best to return the money.

Electrical Appliances

Power sockets are type A and B. Standard voltage is 100v and the frequency is 50 Hz (east) and 60 Hz (west). Adaptors are sold at stores across Tokyo.

Cell Phones and Wi-Fi

With the exception of train stations and some convenience stores, public phones are a rarity. Foreign cell phones may not work in Japan; check coverage with your operator before traveling. If you aren't covered, you can rent a cell phone, SIM card, or Wi-Fi router from companies such as **Softbank Global Rental**. Etiquette requires people to switch their cell phones to silent mode while they are in temples, gardens, and restaurants. Phones should also be switched off near priority seats on public transportation, but this is often ignored.

Major railway stations (all Yamanote Line and many *shinkansen* stations), international airports, hotels, restaurants, convenience store chains, and tourist information centers offer free or inexpensive Wi-Fi.

Postal Services

Yubin-kyoku (post offices) and mailboxes are identified with a character looking like a "T" with an extra horizontal bar across the top. Find your nearest post office on the **Japan Post** website.

Weather

Every season in Tokyo has its attractions, but spring and fall are undoubtedly the most popular, with their blush pink blooms and colorful leaves. They are also the best months for outdoor festivals and cultural events.

The summer months (Jun–late Sep) can be stiflingly hot, with soaring temperatures (100°F/38°C), and high humidity. Typhoons may hit the city in September and October, but these are unpredictable.

Opening Hours

General opening hours for shops are from 10am to 8pm daily, but you'll find many convenience stores also open 24 hours. Restaurants serve lunch between 11.30am and 2.30pm and dinner from 6pm to 10pm. Bars open around 5pm and close in the early hours of the morning. Banks are open 9am to 3pm Monday to Friday, with some open until 5pm. Museums open at 9am or 10am and close around 5pm; most museums and galleries are closed on Monday.

The COVID-19 pandemic proved that situations can change suddenly. Always check before visiting attractions and hospitality venues for up-to-date hours and booking requirements.

Visitor Information

There are several useful Tourist Information Centers (TICs) in Tokyo, including **TIC Tokyo** in Marunouchi, where you should be able to find staff who speak English as well as other languages. These centers can provide maps, leaflets, and itineraries, among other services.

The **Japan National Tourism Organization (JNTO)** has an information office in the Shin-Tokyo Building on Marunouchi's Naka-dori.

Go Tokyo is the city's official tourism information site, available in English. The website of the daily English-language newspaper ***The Japan Times*** has the best local news coverage and international reportage, as well as useful information about what's going on in Tokyo. Useful apps include

HyperDia App, which provides up-to-date information for Japan's rail network, and Yomiwa App, which instantly translates Japanese text.

Local Customs

The traditional greeting in Japan is a bow, its depth reflecting the relative status of participants. Visitors, however, rarely need to bow; a handshake is fine. In many situations, bows are just part of customer service and you do not have to return the bow. If you feel the need to bow, hold your arms and back straight, bend from the waist, and pause at the low point.

Shoes are an important element of etiquette. The principle is not to bring dirt from outside into the interior. Footwear is allowed in hotels, shops, and museums, but there are some places where they are prohibited. You will know when you enter a building or room where shoes are prohibited, as there will usually be a lowered *genkan* (entryway area), where you must take off your shoes and put on slippers. If no slippers are provided, or if they are too small, you can wear socks. No footwear – even slippers – should be worn on tatami matting.

Historically, tattoos have been associated with *yakuza* (mafia) and some *onsen* don't allow people with tattoos. In the run up to the Olympics, the Japanese government implemented measures to ensure that people with tattoos would be able to use hot springs and public baths, but it's still good to check with individual onsen.

There are several rules to be observed when using chopsticks. If you touch food in a communal dish with your chopsticks, you should then take it. Gesturing and pointing with them is seen as bad manners, and it is taboo to pass food from one set of chopsticks to another, as this is associated with funerary rites.

Bodily emissions are considered very rude, though anything drawn inward is acceptable – therefore, sniffing is fine, but blowing your nose in public is not.

Language

Japanese is the official language spoken in Tokyo. The city is well signposted in English, and it is not hard for visitors to find their way around. Many Japanese people speak a little English.

Taxes and Refunds

All visitors must pay a ¥1,000 tourist departure tax. A consumption tax of 10 per cent is charged on goods and services; claiming this money back is a relatively simple process. You can apply for a cash refund as soon as you have made your purchase, at one of the tax refund counters found in department stores (passport required).

Accommodation

In addition to Western-style hotels, Tokyo offers a few idiosyncratic options. *Ryokans* are traditional inns, which may have an on-site *onsen*, while capsule hotels are made up of inexpensive, modern sleeping pods.

For more about the types of accommodation available, visit **Japan National Tourism Organization**. For bookings, try **Japanican** or **Rakuten Travel**.

DIRECTORY

CELL PHONES AND WI-FI

Softbank Global Rental
W softbank-rental.jp

POSTAL SERVICES

Japan Post
W post.japanpost.jp/english

VISITOR INFORMATION

Go Tokyo
W gotokyo.org/en

Japan National Tourism Organization (JNTO)
T 3201-3331
W japan.travel/en

The Japan Times
W japantimes.co.jp

TIC Tokyo
W tictokyo.jp/en

Tokyo Tourist Information Center
T 5321-3077

ACCOMMODATION

Japanican
W japanican.com/en

Japan National Tourism Organization
W japan.travel/en

Rakuten Travel
W travel.rakuten.com

Places to Stay

PRICE CATEGORIES
For a standard, double room per night (with breakfast if included), taxes and extra charges.

¥ under ¥15,000 ¥¥15,000–35,000 ¥¥¥ over ¥35,000

Luxury Hotels

Aman Tokyo
MAP M2 ■ 1-5-6 Otemachi, Chiyoda ■ 5224-3333 ■ www.aman.com ■ ¥¥¥
Located at the top of the Otemachi Tower, in the heart of the financial district, this luxury chain hotel brings its sophisticated calm and style to Tokyo with a serene spa, a swimming pool with great city views, and traditional Japanese touches to the room decor. It also houses fine restaurants and bars.

Andaz Hotel
MAP L5 ■ 1-23-4, Toranomon, Minato ■ 6830-1234 ■ www.hyatt.com ■ ¥¥¥
Part of the Toranomon Hills complex, the Andaz offers real glamour and a great location midway between Roppongi and Ginza. The rooms here are extremely spacious by Tokyo standards and offer panoramic views of the city.

Aoyama Grand Hotel
MAP B5 ■ 2-14-4 Kitaaoyama, Minato ■ www.aoyamagrand.com ■ ¥¥¥
This boutique hotel features "mid-century modern" decor across its rooms and suites. Also on site is a fitness center, plus a range of bars and restaurants including an outlet of the highly acclaimed Kanesaka Sushi.

Grand Hyatt Tokyo
MAP C6 ■ 6-10-3 Roppongi, Minato ■ 4333-1234 ■ www.tokyo.grand.hyatt.com ■ ¥¥¥
Luxurious rooms come with top-grade facilities. All the rooms are tastefully decked out with a combination of natural elements and sleek, contemporary furnishings. Also on-site is an excellent selection of restaurants, a fantastic patisserie, and a spa.

Hoshinoya Tokyo
MAP M2 ■ 1-9-1 Otemachi, Chiyoda ■ hoshinoya.com/tokyo ■ ¥¥¥
The epitome of a contemporary Japanese *ryokan*, this luxury hotel brand's Tokyo outpost has spacious, modern rooms with traditional touches, such as sliding screen doors and tatami flooring. Set in a city-center skyscraper, facilities include an *onsen* on the 17th floor, fed by a source 4,920 ft (1,500 m) below Tokyo.

Hotel Chinzanso
MAP D1 ■ 2-10-8 Sekiguchi, Bunkyo-ku ■ 3943-1111 ■ www.hotel-chinzanso-tokyo.com ■ ¥¥¥
The lobby and corridors of this opulent hotel are decorated with original artwork. Its magnificent Japanese garden has some original features, including a wooden pagoda and Buddhist stone statuary. Rooms are immaculate, albeit on the old-fashioned side.

Imperial Hotel
MAP M4 ■ 1-1-1 Uchisawaicho, Chiyoda ■ 3504-1111 ■ www.imperialhotel.co.jp ■ ¥¥¥
With a history dating from the 1890s, the Imperial Hotel has excellent credentials. Rooms on the Imperial Floor are slightly larger and have the most up-to-date decor. The Imperial's location is also very good: it is set just across from Hibiya Park *(see p81)* and a short stroll away from Ginza.

Mandarin Oriental Tokyo
MAP N2 ■ 2-1-1 Nihonbashimuromachi, Chuo ■ 3270-8800 ■ www.mandarinoriental.com/tokyo ■ ¥¥¥
The Mandarin Oriental oozes luxury. The rooms are decked with Japanese artisan materials, such as paper lanterns, hanging textiles, and traditional furnishings. Panoramic views of Mount Fuji and the Tokyo business district add to the charm. There are also several exceptional bars and restaurants located on site.

The Okura Tokyo
MAP K5 ■ 2-10-4 Toranomon, Minato ■ 3582-0111 ■ www.theokuratokyo.jp ■ ¥¥¥
Okura's main building was reconstructed ahead of the delayed 2020 Olympics,

but this hotel remains as iconic as ever. The lobby here sports a retro style, and the rooms are spacious and comfortable. Other amenities include a fitness center, spa, salon, and several restaurants.

Palace Hotel

MAP M2 ■ 1-1-1 Marunouchi, Chiyoda ■ 3211-5211 ■ en.palacehoteltokyo.com ■ ¥¥¥

Given a makeover in 2012, this is a serenely quiet, classic establishment with spacious rooms. The many excellent restaurants and bars on site leave visitors spoilt for choice. Counting the Japanese emperor as a neighbor, the Palace Hotel also offers great views of the Imperial Palace *(see pp12–13)*.

Park Hyatt Tokyo

MAP A4 ■ 3-7-1-2 Nishishinjuku, Shinjuku ■ www.hyatt.com ■ ¥¥¥

The ritzy Park Hyatt was the setting for the movie *Lost in Translation*, which features Scarlett Johansson. It offers stellar views across the city, especially at night. The spa and the magnificent swimming pool are in a class of their own. Expect superb service and first-class bars and restaurants.

Peninsula Hotel Tokyo

MAP M4 ■ 1-8-1 Yurakucho, Chiyoda ■ 6270-2888 ■ www.peninsula.com/en/tokyo ■ ¥¥¥

Completed in 2008, this reputed 24-story hotel overlooks the Imperial Palace East Gardens *(see p12)* and Hibiya Park *(see p50)*. Shopping in Ginza and Marunouchi is a short stroll away.

Ritz-Carlton

MAP D5 ■ Tokyo Midtown, 9-7-1 Akasaka, Minato ■ 3423-8000 ■ www.ritzcarlton.com ■ ¥¥¥

Set close to the Roppongi entertainment area, the sumptuous Ritz-Carlton has spellbinding views, outstanding bars and restaurants, and world-class amenities. As you would expect of a hotel of this class, the service is second to none.

Shangri-La Hotel

MAP N3 ■ Marunouchi Trust Tower Main, 1-8-3 Marunouchi, Chiyoda ■ 6739-7888 ■ www.shangri-la.com/tokyo ■ ¥¥¥

Located next to Tokyo Station, the Shangri-La offers guests handsomely appointed rooms that look out over striking cityscape vistas. Visitors will find impeccable service here, plus excellent facilities.

The Strings by InterContinental Tokyo

MAP C2 ■ Shinagawa East One Tower, 26-32F, 2-16-1 Konan, Minato ■ 5783-1111 ■ www.intercontinental-strings.jp ■ ¥¥¥

Spread across the 26th to 32nd floors, the hotel has scenic views of Odaiba Island *(see pp34–5)* and Rainbow Bridge *(see p34)*. The rooms are flooded with natural light thanks to their large windows and feature modern furniture in muted colors, with comfortable low-slung sofas.

The Tokyo Edition, Toranomon

MAP E5 ■ 4-1-1 Toranomon, Minato ■ www.marriott.com ■ ¥¥¥

Located near Tokyo Tower and Roppongi, the Edition features Kengo Kuma-designed interiors that are natural in tone and minimal in style. You'll also find a pool, spa, and fitness center on site.

Mid-Range Hotels

Cerulean Tower Tokyu Hotel

MAP R6 ■ 26-1 Sakuragaokacho, Shibuya ■ 3476-3000 ■ www.tokyuhotels.co.jp/cerulean-h ■ ¥¥

Shibuya's premier luxury hotel offers huge rooms, stylish interiors, *kaiseki* restaurants, bars, a jazz club, and a traditional Noh theater. The best rooms for breathtaking views are those between the 31st and 37th floors.

Hyatt Centric Ginza

MAP F5 ■ 6-6-7 Ginza, Chuo ■ www.hyatt.com ■ ¥¥

Japan's first Centric, opened in 2018, enjoys a great location in the heart of Ginza. It has minimal facilities compared to other Hyatt branches, but the rooms and suites here are spacious and stylish. There is also an on-site fitness center and a bar-lounge that is perfect for unwinding.

Hilltop Hotel

MAP E3 ■ 1-1 Kandasurugadai, Chiyoda ■ 3293-2311 ■ www.yamanoue-hotel.co.jp ■ ¥¥

An old favorite with Tokyo writers, this pre-war Art Deco hotel exudes charm and character. The older rooms are furnished with old-fashioned writing desks, while the more expensive suites have small private gardens.

For a key to hotel price categories *see p128*

Hotel Niwa Tokyo

MAP E3 ■ 1-1-16 Kandamisakicho, Chiyoda ■ 3293-0028 ■ www.hotelniwa.jp ■ ¥¥

For a bargain price, this central hotel has much to offer, including a rooftop garden and two restaurants. The good-sized rooms feature modern Japanese decor; some also have balconies and city views.

Keio Plaza Hotel

MAP A4 ■ 2-2-1 Nishishinjuku, Shinjuku ■ 3344-0111 ■ www.keioplaza.com ■ ¥¥

One of the best bases for visiting the sights of Shinjuku. Room rates here are reasonable, given its location among the skyscrapers of West Shinjuku and its first-rate amenities, which include several restaurants, stores, and an outdoor pool.

Mitsui Garden Hotel Ginza Premier

MAP M5 ■ 8-13-1 Ginza, Chuo ■ 3543-1131 ■ www.gardenhotels.co.jp ■ ¥¥

Located in Ginza, this modern skyscraper hotel offers four-star luxury and beautiful views at a reasonable price. There are other Mitsui Garden hotels nearby.

Sequence Miyashita Park

MAP Q5 ■ 6-20-10 Jingumae, Shibuya ■ www.sequencehotels.com/miyashita-park ■ ¥¥

This stylish hangout overlooks the new Miyashita Park development. The sleek accommodation options range from suites to bunk rooms.

Budget Hotels

Asia Center of Japan

MAP C5 ■ 8-10-32 Akasaka, Minato ■ 3402-6111 ■ www.asiacenter.or.jp ■ ¥

Set in fashionable Aoyama, the Asia Center offers all the facilities of a business hotel at affordable rates. Rooms are basic but reasonably spacious.A free buffet breakfast is available to overseas guests and staff all speak English.

Book and Bed Shinjuku

MAP B3 ■ 1-27-5 Kabukicho, Shinjuku ■ www.bookandbedtokyo.com/en/shinjuku ■ ¥

At this trendy hostel, the beds are cosy cubby holes built to fit into well-stocked bookcases. There are private superior doubles available too.

Granbell Hotel

MAP B6 ■ 15-17 Sakuragaokacho, Shibuya ■ 5457-2681 ■ www.granbellhotel.jp ■ ¥

This cheerful hotel is a short walk from Shibuya Station. Double and single rooms have simple furnishings. There is also an excellent, maisonette-style terrace suite.

Hotel Monterey Hanzomon

MAP K2 ■ 23-1 Ichibancho, Chiyoda ■ 3556-7111 ■ www.hotelmonterey.co.jp ■ ¥

The rooms here blend contemporary architecture with traditional Japanese design, while the wall colors reflect the tastes of samurai residences of the Edo period.

Khaosan Tokyo Laboratory

MAP Q3 ■ 2-1-4 Nishiasakusa, Taito ■ 6479-1041 ■ www.khaosan-tokyo.com/en ■ ¥

Perfect for families, this hostel has a range of vividly painted rooms with a double and single bed, as well as dorms sleeping four, all of which have en suite bathrooms. There are several other branches in Tokyo.

K's House Tokyo

MAP R3 ■ 3-20-10 Kuramae, Taito ■ 5833-0555 ■ www.kshouse.jp/tokyo-e ■ ¥

Set in a yellow-painted building a short walk south of Asakusa, this comfortable hostel has a mix of dorms and private rooms, a roof terrace, and a pleasant lounge, where you can hang out and meet fellow travelers.

Nui

MAP R3 ■ 2-14-13 Kuramae, Taito ■ 6240-9854 ■ www.backpackersjapan.co.jp/nuihostel ■ ¥

From the Toco team comes this hip hostel in a converted warehouse. High-ceilinged dormitories and private rooms share the communal bathrooms while on the ground floor is a popular café-bar that attracts the area's creatives.

Sakura Hotel

MAP L1 ■ 2-21-4 Kandajinbocho, Chiyoda ■ 3261-3939 ■ www.sakura-hotel.co.jp ■ ¥

A popular choice with budget-range travelers, the Sakura Hotel offers accommodation options comprising shared dorms and minuscule, but cozy, private rooms, all non-smoking. The English-speaking staff are very friendly, and the hotel's good location is a bonus.

Shinjuku Kuyakusho-mae Capsule Hotel
MAP B3 ■ 1-2-5 Kabukicho, Shinjuku ■ 3232-1110 ■ www.capsuleinn.com/shinjuku/en ■ ¥
Offering perfect access to the Shinjuku area, this inexpensive, clean capsule hotel is just a four-minute walk from the station. There are separate capsule floors for men and women.

Toco
MAP G1 ■ 2-13-21 Shitaya, Taito ■ 6458-1686 ■ www.backpackersjapan.co.jp/toco ■ ¥
A geisha used to live in this lovely 1920s wooden building, which has been converted into a cool hostel. There are small dorms and a handful of private Japanese-style rooms. The hostel also has a serene Japanese garden and a pleasant lounge bar.

Tokyo Central Youth Hostel
MAP B3 ■ Central Plaza 18F, 1-1 Kaguragashi, Shinjuku ■ 3235-1107 ■ www.jyh.gr.jp/tcyh/eng ■ ¥
A modern hostel on the 18th and 19th floors of Central Plaza. Except for a Japanese-style family room, accommodation is in shared dorms. Other features include a souvenir store, dining hall, Internet access, and a TV in the lobby.

Tokyo Hütte
MAP D1 ■ 4-18-16 Narihira, Sumida ■ 5637-7628 ■ www.tokyohutte.co.jp/en ■ ¥
Across the Sumida River *(see pp16–17)* from the district of Asakusa and within a stone's throw of Tokyo Skytree *(see p89)* is this stylish new hostel. The mixed and female-only dorms offer extra-wide beds screened off by curtains to ensure privacy and there are private Japanese-style rooms, plus a co-working space.

Rooms with a View

Asakusa View Hotel
MAP Q2 ■ 3-17-1 Nishiasakusa, Taito ■ 3847-1111 ■ www.viewhotels.co.jp/asakusa ■ ¥
As the name suggests, the views of neighboring rooftops and the nearby Senso-ji Temple *(see pp14–15)* from these comfortable Western-style rooms are of a charming older Tokyo. The bar on the 28th floor offers visitors the best views of the Sumida River and the nearby Tokyo Skytree tower.

Hilton Tokyo Odaiba
MAP D2 ■ 1-9-1 Daiba, Minato ■ 5500-5500 ■ www.hilton.com ■ ¥¥
This well-appointed hotel is located next to the Tokyo Decks mall, near the Odaiba Marine Park *(see p35)* with its artificial beach and copy of the Statue of Liberty. Its luxurious rooms offer stunning vistas of the bay, island, and waterfront.

InterContinental Tokyo Bay
MAP C1 ■ 1-16-2 Kaigan, Minato ■ 5404-2222 ■ www.interconti-tokyo.com ■ ¥¥
The views from the stylish rooms here are truly panoramic. Large windows face the Sumida River, the Tokyo Skytree observation tower, the wharves of Tokyo Bay, and Rainbow Bridge, which links the city to Odaiba Island *(see pp34–5)*. There are several dining options available on site. The 20th-floor lounge bar offers truly amazing views of the bridge when it is illuminated after dark.

Shinjuku Prince Hotel
MAP B3 ■ 1-30-1 Kabukicho, Shinjuku ■ 3205-1111 ■ www.princehotels.co.jp ■ ¥¥
Next to JR Shinjuku Station, this high-rise hotel offers incredible views of the Kabukicho entertainment zone from guest rooms and its 25th-floor restaurant. Good facilities and reasonably sized rooms.

Conrad Hotel
MAP M6 ■ 1-9-1 Higashishinbashi, Minato ■ 6388-8000 ■ conrad-tokyo.hiltonjapan.co.jp ■ ¥¥¥
The cityscape views and aerial perspectives of lush Hama Rikyu Garden *(see p50)* from this 37-story luxury hotel are unparalleled. Aromatic therapies, cedar wood spas, and superb cuisine will all contribute to a memorable stay.

***For a key to hotel price categories** see p128*

Four Seasons Hotel Tokyo at Marunouchi

MAP N3 ■ Pacific Century Place, 1-11-1 Marunouchi, Chiyoda ■ 5222-7222 ■ www.fourseasons.com/tokyo ■ ¥¥¥

Located close to Tokyo Station and the Imperial Palace *(see pp12–13)*, this luxurious hotel has large rooms equipped with 3-D/Blu-ray built-in TVs, and offers great views of central Tokyo. The service extended by the hotel's multilingual staff is impeccable.

Tokyo Station Hotel

MAP N3 ■ 1-9-1 Marunouchi, Chiyoda ■ 5220-1111 ■ www.tokyostationhotel.jp ■ ¥¥¥

Occupying one wing of the original 1914, red-brick Tokyo Station *(see p76)* building, this beautifully appointed hotel has been given a recent update. You can watch the *shinkansen* trains at the station or gaze out at the towers of Marunouchi and Ginza.

The Westin Tokyo

MAP C2 ■ 1-4-1 Mita, Meguro ■ 5423-7000 ■ www.marriott.co.jp/hotels/travel/tyowi-the-westin-tokyo ■ ¥¥¥

Styled along the lines of grand European hotels, the Westin stands just beyond the Ebisu Garden Place complex. Views from the middle and upper rooms toward the bay and inward over the city are stunning.

Ryokan and Minsuku

Andon Ryokan

MAP H1 ■ 2-34-10 Nihon-zutsumi, Taito ■ 3873-8611 ■ www.andon.co.jp ■ ¥

Enjoy the owner's antique collection while taking in the compact design of this modern *ryokan*. Every room has Internet access, a TV, and a DVD player. All floors have showers. There is also a communal Jacuzzi. The staff speak English.

Hotel Fukudaya

MAP C2 ■ 4-5-9 Aobadai, Meguro ■ 3467-5833 ■ www2.gol.com/users/ryokan-fukudaya ■ ¥

There's a set of samurai armor displayed in the lobby of this small family-run inn, which is within walking distance of Naka-Meguro and Shibuya. Most of the rooms are traditional with futon beds and tatami-mat floors. Communal bathroom.

Kimi Ryokan

MAP C1 ■ 2-36-8 Ikebukuro, Toshima ■ 3971-3766 ■ www.kimi-ryokan.jp ■ ¥

Popular with budget travelers, this inn offers small but immaculate Japanese rooms. Bathing is communal. The place offers great value, so it is advisable to book ahead.

Ryokan Katsutaro

MAP F1 ■ 4-16-8 Ikeno-hata, Taito ■ 3821-9808 ■ www.katsutaro.com ■ ¥

Seven Japanese-style rooms are provided at this friendly, family-run *ryokan* in a quiet, traditional district near Ueno Park *(see pp20–21)*. It also has an annex in Yanaka.

Ryokan Sansuiso

MAP D2 ■ 2-9-5 Higashigotanda, Shinagawa ■ 3441-7475 ■ www.sansuiso.net ■ ¥

An affordable choice close to Gotanda Station. Some of the Japanese rooms have baths, others have communal facilities. Note that there is a midnight curfew and credit cards are not accepted.

Ryokan Shigetsu

MAP R3 ■ 1-31-11 Asakusa, Taito ■ 3843-2345 ■ www.shigetsu.com ■ ¥

This beautifully maintained *ryokan* is adorned with paper screen windows and tatami mats. The two traditional baths here are a highlight, with views respectively of Senso-ji Temple and the city itself.

Sawanoya Ryokan

MAP F1 ■ 2-3-11 Yanaka, Taito ■ 3822-2251 ■ www.sawanoya.com ■ ¥

A long-established *ryokan* popular with foreign guests. Rooms are small, but comfortable. There's a communal tub but some rooms do have en suite baths. It is set in Yanaka, close to Ueno Park *(see p20–21)*. Credit cards are not accepted.

Tokyo Ryokan

MAP Q3 ■ 2-4-8 Nishiasakusa, Taito ■ 090-8879-3599 ■ www.tokyoryokan.com ■ ¥

Ideal for exploring Asakusa, this charming traditional place, with just three rooms, has commu-nal bathing. No meals are provided, but there are many restaurants situated nearby.

Further Afield

Annex Turtle Hotori-an

MAP B1 ■ 8-28 Takumicho, Nikko ■ 0288-53-3663 ■ www.turtle-nikko.com ■ ¥

This accommodation with English-speaking staff has been welcoming travelers to Nikko for decades. This is the more modern annex to their original guesthouse and has both Western and Japanese style rooms. The inn is at a convenient distance to UNESCO World Heritage Sites such as the Toshogu shrine.

Fuji Hakone Guest House

MAP A2 ■ 912 Sengokuhara, Hakone ■ 0460-84-6577 ■ www.fujihakone.com ■ ¥

This traditional-style inn is run by an English-speaking family. They are very welcoming and very knowledgeable about the area's attractions. Sleep on a futon and soak in an outdoor *onsen* bath.

Hotel New Grand

MAP B2 ■ 10 Yamashitacho, Naka, Yokohama ■ 045-681-1841 ■ www.hotel-newgrand.co.jp ■ ¥¥

A historic hotel in Japan's second-largest city, the Grand occupies a prime spot opposite a waterfront park and the contemporary cruise terminal. The public areas of the original building live up to their grand billing.

Hotel New Kamakura

MAP B2 ■ 13-2 Onarimachi, Kamakura ■ 0467-22-2230 ■ www.newkamakura.com ■ ¥¥

Close by the station, the New Kamakura is actually one of the temple town's oldest Western-style hotels with plenty of retro charm. Rooms, both Western and Japanese style, are split across two small buildings.

Nine Hours Narita Airport

MAP B2 ■ Narita International Airport Terminal 2, 1-1 Furugome, Narita ■ 0476-33-5109 ■ www.ninehours.co.jp/narita ■ ¥

Handy both for Tokyo's main international airport and as an affordable base for the attractions of Narita. Guests sleep in a roomy, state-of-the art capsule. Luggage lockers and communal shower facilities for men and women are available.

Fuji Lake Hotel

MAP A2 ■ 1 Funatsu, Fujikawaguchiko ■ 0555-72-2209 ■ www.fujilake.co.jp ■ ¥¥

Stunningly located on the clear shores of Lake Kawaguchi with Mount Fuji as its backdrop, this 1930s hotel has bags of retro appeal. There is a sauna and Jacuzzi in the communal *onsen* bathroom and a viewing terrace if your room does not face Mount Fuji.

Fujiya Hotel

MAP B2 ■ 359 Miyanoshita, Hakone ■ 0460-82-2211 ■ www.fujiyahotel.jp ■ ¥¥¥

One of the oldest Western hotels in Japan and a true classic, the Fujiya has been in business since 1878, and the wonderful old building has drawn countless dignitaries and celebrities from around the world, including John Lennon. The hotel offers four types of accommodation and the main dining room is simply majestic. All rooms have a bath fed by natural hot springs.

Nikko Kanaya Hotel

MAP B1 ■ 1300 Kamihatsuishimachi, ■ 0288-54-0001 ■ www.kanayahotel.co.jp ■ ¥¥¥

Built in 1873, this classic resort hotel presents an impressive blend of old-world charm and flawless service. Well-appointed rooms date from the Meiji era to the 1950s.

Yokohama Royal Park Hotel

MAP B2 ■ 2-2-1-3 Minato Mirai, Nishi, Yokohama ■ 045-221-1111 ■ www.yrph.com ■ ¥¥

This hotel is ideal for those looking for great views. Rooms are located on the 52nd to 67th floors of the soaring Landmark Tower, offering a splendid vista of the waterfront and Mount Fuji.

Hoshinoya Fuji

MAP A2 ■ 1408 Oishi, Fujikawaguchiko ■ www.hoshinoya.com/fuji/en ■ ¥¥¥

Japan's first glamping resort, Hoshinoya Fuji is as far from camping as you could imagine. Stay in stylish, minimalist cabins, eat under the stars and take part in a range of activities around the lake and Mount Fuji.

General Index

Page numbers in **bold** refer to main entries

21_21 Design Sight 49, 95, 97
47 Ronin Incident (1701) 38, 42
3331 Arts Chiyoda 47

A
Ad Museum Tokyo 45, 83
Air travel 120
Akasaka *see* Roppongi and Akasaka
Akihito, Emperor 13
Ambulances 125
Ameyoko Market 6, 67
Amuse Museum 89
Amusement parks
  Hanayashiki 88, 89
  Tokyo Disney® Resort 55, 116
  Tokyo Dome City 55
Ando, Tadao 51, 95, 101, 103
Aoyama, Harajuku, and Shibuya **100–105**
  fashion and design hangouts 104
  maps 100, 103
  restaurants 105
  walk 103
Aoyama Cemetery 101
Aqua City 35
Archery, horseback 70
Architecture 68
  Edo-Tokyo Open Air Architectural Museum 114–15
  modern and contemporary buildings 50–51
Art
  arts stores 67
  public art 68
  art galleries 46–7
  Roppongi street art 96
  see also Museums and galleries
Asahara, Shoko 39
Asahi Beer Hall 16, 48
Asakura, Fumio 33
Asakura Museum of Sculpture 33
Asakusa *see* Ueno, Asakusa, and Oshiage
Asakusa Engei Hall 59, 89
Asakusa Jinja 15
Asano, Lord 38
ATMs 126
Audi Forum Tokyo 103
Aum Shinrikyo subway attack (1995) 39
Azekura Sutra Store 26
Azumabashi Bridge 89

B
Babasaki Moat 77
Bank of Japan 40, 75, 76
Banks 126
Bars 64–5
  budget tips 69
  opening hours 126
  Roppongi and Akasaka 98
  Shinjuku 110
Basho, Matsuo 17
Basho Inari Shrine and Statue 17
Baths and hot springs 34, 60–61
Battery Islands 34
Benten-do 21
Benten Mound 15
Bertolucci, Bernardo 39
Bicycles 122–3
"Black ships" 38, 114
Boats 123
Bourgeois, Louise 96, 97
Bridges
  Azumabashi Bridge 89
  Eitai Bridge 17
  Engetsukyo Bridge 28
  JR Bridge 31
  Kiyosu Bridge 16
  Komagata Bridge 16
  Nihonbashi Bridge 18, 76
  Nijubashi Bridge 12
  Rainbow Bridge 34
  Tsutenkyo Bridge 29
  Umaya Bridge 17
  Yanagi Bridge 16
Budget travel
  free events 68–9
  hotels 130–31
Budokan 77
Bunka Gakuen Costume Museum 107
Bunkamura Theater 58
Buses 120, 122

C
Cafés 64–5
  themed 53
Canadian Embassy Garden 50
Caretta Shiodome 83
Cars, driving in Tokyo 123
Cathedrals
  Nikolai Cathedral 41, 43
  St. Mary's Cathedral 49
Cell phones 126
Cemeteries
  Aoyama Cemetery 101
  Yanaka Cemetery 32
Central Tokyo **74–9**
  maps 74, 77
  restaurants 79
  shopping 78
  walk 77
Cherry blossom 21, 71
Chidorigafuchi 13
Children's attractions 54–5
Cinema *see* Film
Clock Museum, Daimyo 33
Clothes
  Bunka Gakuen Costume Museum 107
  shopping 104
Coming-of-Age Day 71
Conder, Josiah 40, 43
Confucianism 42
Coppola, Sofia 59
Covid-19 126
Credit cards 126
Crime 124–5
Cultural phenomena 57
Currency 126
Currency Museum 76
Customs information 124
Cycling 122–3

D
Daikanyama 52
Decks Tokyo Beach 35
Denbo-in Garden 15
Design Festa 70
DiverCity Tokyo Plaza 35
Doctors 124
Drum Museum 54

E
Earthquakes 13, 38, 124
Edo 38
Edo Castle 76
Edo Taito Traditional Crafts Center 88, 89
Edo-Tokyo Museum 44
Edo-Tokyo Open Air Architectural Museum 40, 114–15
Eitai Bridge 17
Electrical appliances 126
Emergency services 125
Ende and Böckmann 41
Engetsukyo Bridge 28
Enshu, Kobori 15, 75
Entertainment 58–9
  festivals and events 69, 70–71
  free events 68–9
  pop culture venues 56–7
Ethnic food, Shin-Okubo 108
Events 69, 70–71

F
Farther afield **112–17**
  The Best of the Rest 116
  hotels 133
  map 112–13
  restaurants 117

Farther afield (cont.)
Two days in Kamakura 115
Ferries 123
Festivals 69, 70–71
Films 59
National Film Archive (NFAJ) 81
Fire services 125
Fireworks, Sumida River 17, 71
Flea markets 69
Flower and plant events 71
Food and drink
ethnic food in Shin-Okubo 108
see also Bars; Cafés; Restaurants
Free events 68–9
Fuji, Mount 114
Fuji TV Building 35, 48
Fujita, Tsuguharu 12

G

Galleries *see* Museums and galleries
Gallery Koyanagi 46
Gallery Ma 97
Gardens *see* Parks and gardens
Ghibli Museum 54, 57, 116
Ginza 69, **80–85**
maps 80, 83
restaurants 85
shopping 83
specialist stores 84
walk 83
Ginza Graphic Gallery 46
Gojo Tenjin Fox Shrine 20
Gokuku-ji Temple 41
Golden Gai 7, 107, 109
Golden Kannon 15, 38
Gotoh Art Museum 116
Government advice 124
Grant, Ulysses S. 43
Great Buddha of Yanaka 32, 33
Great Kanto Earthquake (1923) 13, 38
Great Wave (Hokusai) 39

H

Hachiko
statue of 69, 101, 102
Hakone 114
Hamarikyu Garden 6, 17, 50, 82
Hanayashiki 88, 89
Hanazari Inari Fox Shrine 20
Hanazono Shrine 109
Haneda Airport 120–21
Harajuku *see* Aoyama, Harajuku, and Shibuya
Hattori Building 41, 83
Health care 124
Heiseikan 26
Herzog & de Meuron 51
Hibiya Park 50, 81
Hie Shrine 43, 92–3, 95
Higuchi, Ichiyo 39
Historic buildings 40–41
History 38–9
Hokusai, Katsushika 39, 101
Hongan-ji Temple 40
Honkan 26
Horai-jima Island 28
Horseback archery 70
Hospitals 124
Hot springs 34, 60–61
Hotels 127, 128–33
Hyokeikan 27

I

Ichi no Torii 30
Idemitsu, Sado 82
Idemitsu Museum of Arts 45, 82
Ienari 82
Ietsuna 82
Ikebukuro 52
Imperial Palace East Gardens 12, 75, 77
Imperial Palace Grounds 6, 7, 10, **12–13**
Imperial Palace Plaza 13
Inari 42
Inokashira Park 116
Institute for Nature Study and Park 51
Insurance 124
Intermediatheque 44, 76
Internet 69, 126
Isetan Art Gallery 109
Isetatsu 33
Ito, Chuta 40
Ito, Toyo 101, 103
Izumi, Yosuke 88

J

Japanese Sword Museum 53
Japan Sake and Shochu Information Center 81
Jenner, Edward, statue of 27
Jindaiji Temple 116
Joypolis 34, 54
JR Bridge 31

K

Kabuki-za Theater 6, 59, 81
Kabukicho 7, 106, 109
Kagurazaka 53
Kamakura 115
Kaminari-mon Gate 14, 89
Kanda Matsuri 71
Kanda Myojin Shrine 42
Kannon 14, 15, 38, 70
Kappabashi Kitchenware Town 89
Kara-mon Gate 20
Kassatkin, St. Nikolai 43
Kawagoe 113
Kawaguchi-ko 114
Kenzo Tange Associates 50
KidZania 54
Kikuchi, Rinko 59
Kikuchi, Tomo 96
Kira, Lord 38
Kitanomaru Park 77
Kite Museum 54, 77
Kiyosu Bridge 16
Kiyosumi Garden 50
Koishikawa Koraku-en Garden 7, 11, **28–9**, 51
Komagata Bridge 16
Kotozan Daien-ji Temple 32
Korin, Ogata 100
Kuhachiya House 28
Kuma, Kengo 44, 53, 103
Kuramae 52
Kurokawa, Kisho 50, 51
Kurosawa, Akira 39
Kyu-Furukawa Gardens 52
Kyu Iwasaki-tei Mansion 40

L

Language, phrase book 141–3
Le Corbusier 20
Long-Sleeves Fire (1657) 38

M

Maekawa, Kunio 87
Maki, Fumihiko 46
Manet, Édouard 75
Manjiro, John 101
Maps
Aoyama, Harajuku, and Shibuya 100, 103
art galleries 46
cafés and bars 64
Central Tokyo 74, 77
exploring Tokyo 6–7
Farther afield 112–13
gardens and parks 48
Ginza 80, 83
historic buildings 41
Imperial Palace Grounds 13
Kamakura 115
Koishikawa Koraku-en Garden 51
modern and contemporary buildings 50
museums and galleries 44
Odaiba Island 35
places of worship 43
restaurants 63
Roppongi and Akasaka 94, 97
Senso-ji Temple 15
Shinjuku 106, 109

Maps (cont.)
Tokyo highlights 10–11
Ueno, Asakusa, and Oshiage 86–7, 89
Ueno Park 21
Markets 66–7, 69
Marunouchi 76
Meiji Emperor 30, 43, 95, 102
Meiji era 21
Meiji Jingu Museum 30
Meiji Jingu Shrine 6, 7, 11, **30–31**, 43, 102
Meiji Jingu Shrine Iris Garden 11, 31
Michiko, Empress 13
Ministry of Justice Building 41
Minsuku, hotels 132–3
Mitford, Algernon 30
Mito family 29
Mitsui Memorial Museum 77
Miyake, Issey 95
Miyazaki, Hayao 39, 54, 116
Mobile phones 126
Mode Gakuen Cocoon Tower 48
Modern and contemporary buildings 50–51
Money 126
Monorail 120
Mori Art Museum 45, 97
Mount Fuji 114
Mount Takao 114
Mukojima Hyakka-en Garden 50
Murray, Bill 59
Museums and galleries 44–7
budget tips 68, 69
3331 Arts Chiyoda 47
Ad Museum Tokyo 45, 83
Amuse Museum 89
Asakura Museum of Sculpture 33
Bunka Gakuen Costume Museum 107
Currency Museum opening hours 126
Drum Museum 54
Edo Taito Traditional Crafts Center 88, 89
Edo-Tokyo Museum 44
Edo-Tokyo Open Air Architectural Museum 114–15
Gallery Koyanagi 46
Gallery Ma 97
Ghibli Museum 54, 57, 116
Ginza Graphic Gallery 46
Gotoh Art Museum 116
Idemitsu Museum of Arts 45, 82
Intermediatheque 44, 76
Isetan Art Gallery 109
Museums and galleries (cont.)
Japanese Sword Museum 53
Kite Museum 54, 77
Meiji Jingu Museum 30
Mitsui Memorial Museum 77
Mori Art Museum 45, 97
Mukojima Hyakka-en Garden 50
Musée Tomo 96
Museum of Contemporary Art (MOT) 116
National Art Center, Tokyo 47, 49, 95, 97
National Film Archive of Japan (NFAJ) 81
National Museum of Emerging Science and Innovation 7, 35, 55
National Museum of Modern Art (MOMAT) 6, 12, 75
National Museum of Nature and Science 55, 87
National Museum of Western Art 20
Nezu Museum 6, 44, 100, 103
Nihon Minka-en 116
NTT InterCommunication Center 108
Ota Memorial Museum of Art 44, 101
Railway Museum (Omiya) 54, 113
Sannomaru Shozokan 13
SCAI – The Bathhouse 33, 47
Shiseido Gallery 46
Shitamachi Museum 21
Sompo Museum of Art 108
Spiral 46, 103
Suginami Animation Museum 116
Suntory Museum of Art 47, 95, 97
Taka Ishii Gallery 47
Taro Okamoto Memorial Museum 103
Toguri Museum of Art 102
Tokyo Metropolitan Art Museum 87
Tokyo Metropolitan Museum of Photography 45
Tokyo National Museum 6, 7, 11, **24–7**, 45, 87
The Tolman Collection 46
Yayoi Kusama Museum 44

N

Nade Jizo 15
Nagai, Kafu 39
Naka-Meguro 52
Nakamise-dori 14
Nakano 116
Naritasan Shinsho-ji Temple 115
National Art Center, Tokyo 47, 49, 95, 97
National Diet Building 40
National Film Archive of Japan (NFAJ) 81
National Museum of Emerging Science and Innovation 7, 35, 55
National Museum of Modern Art (MOMAT) 6, 12, 75
National Museum of Nature and Science 55, 87
National Museum of Western Art 20
National Noh Theater 58
National Theatre 58
Natsume, Soseki 39
New National Theatre 58
New Year's Day 70
Nezu, Kaichiro 100
Nezu Museum 6, 44, 100, 103
Nezu Shrine 42
Nihon Minka-en 116
Nihonbashi Bridge 18, 76
Nihonbashi 10, **18–19**
Nijubashi Bridge 12
Nikko 113
Nikolai Cathedral 41, 43
Ningyocho 53
Nippon Budokan 13
Nishizawa, Ryue 101
Niten-mon Gate 14
Nogi, General Maresuke 95
Nogi Shrine 95, 97
Noh theater 58
NTT InterCommunication Center 108

O

Odaiba Island 7, 11, **34–5**
Odaiba Marine Park 35
Oden, Takahashi 32
Off the beaten path 52–3
Okamoto, Taro 103
Olympic Games (1964) 39, 76, 102
Omiya 113
Omotesando 6, 7, 101, 103
Ono, Yoko 39
Onsen 60–61
Opening hours 126
Origami Kaikan 69
Oshiage *see* Ueno, Asakusa, and Oshiage
Oshima, Nagisa 59
Ota Memorial Museum of Art 44, 101

Ota, Seizo 101
Ota Dokan's Castle 38
Ote-mon Gate 12
Ozu, Yasujiro 39, 59

P

Palace *see* Imperial Palace
Parkes, Sir Harry 30
Parks and gardens 48–9
  Denbo-in Garden 15
  flower and plant events 71
  Hamarikyu Garden 6, 17, 50, 82
  Hibiya Park 50, 81
  Imperial Palace East Gardens 12, 75, 77
  Imperial Palace Grounds 6, 7, 10, **12–13**
  Inokashira Park 116
  Institute for Nature Study and Park 51
  Kitanomaru Park 77
  Kiyosumi Garden 50
  Koishikawa Koraku-en Garden 7, 11, **28–9**, 51
  Kyu-Furukawa Gardens 52
  Meiji Jingu Shrine Iris Garden 11, 31
  Odaiba Marine Park 35
  Rikugi-en Garden 51
  Shinjuku Gyoen 36–7, 51, 107, 109
  Tokyo National Museum 26
  Ueno Park 6, 7, 10, **20–21**, 86
  Wadakura Fountain Park 13
  Yoyogi Park 51, 68–9
Parliament 40
Passports 124
Perry, Commodore Matthew 34, 38, 114
Personal security 124–5
Pharmacies 124
Phrase book 141–3
Places of worship 42–3
Police 125
Pop culture venues 56–7
Postal services 126
Prada Aoyama Building 49
Public art 68

R

Railways 120, 121
  Railway Museum (Omiya) 54, 113
Rainbow Bridge 34
Religion 42–3
Restaurants 62–3
  Aoyama, Harajuku, and Shibuya 105
  budget tips 69
  Central Tokyo 79
  Farther afield 117
  Ginza 85
Restaurants (cont.)
  opening hours 126
  Roppongi and Akasaka 99
  Shinjuku 111
  Ueno, Asakusa, and Oshiage 91
  see also Food and drink
Rickshaws 88
Rikugi-en Garden 51
RiSuPia 34
Roppongi and Akasaka **94–9**
  bars 98
  maps 94, 97
  restaurants 99
  street art 96
  walk 97
Roppongi Hills 6, 94, 97
Russian Orthodox Church 41, 43
Ryogoku 53
Ryokan and Minsuku hotels 132–3

S

Safety 124, 125
Saigo Takamori Statue 21
Sannomaru Shozokan 13
Sanrio Puroland 56
St. Mary's Cathedral 49
Sakamoto, Ryuichi 39
Sakurada-mon Gate 12
San-mon Gate 97
Sanja Festival 70
SCAI – The Bathhouse 33, 47
Sejima, Kazuyo 101
Sengaku-ji Temple 42
Senso-ji Temple 6, 7, 8–9, 10, **14–15**, 38, 42, 88, 89
Sento 60–61
Seven-Five-Three Festival 71
Sharaku, Toshusai 101
Shibamata 116
Shibuya *see* Aoyama, Harajuku, and Shibuya
Shibuya Crossing 69, 103
Shibuya style 103
Shimokitazawa 52
Shinbashi Enbujo 59
Shin-Okubo 108, 109
Shinjuku 6, 72–3, **106–11**
  bars 110
  maps 106, 109
  restaurants 111
  walk 109
Shinjuku Gyoen 36–7, 51, 107, 109
Shinobazu Pond 21
Shinto architecture 30
Shiodome 83
Shiomizaka 12
Shiseido Gallery 46
Shitamachi Museum 21
Shoken, Empress 30
Shopping
  Aoyama, Harajuku, and Shibuya 104
  Central Tokyo 78
  children's shopping 55
  Ginza 83, 84
  markets, shopping streets, and stores 66–7
  opening hours 126
  Ueno, Asakusa, and Oshiage 90
Shrines 68
  Basho Inari Shrine and Statue 17
  Gojo Tenjin Fox Shrine 20
  Hanazari Inari Fox Shrine 20
  Hanazono Shrine 109
  Hie Shrine 43, 92–3, 95
  Kanda Myojin Shrine 42
  Meiji Jingu Shrine 6, 7, 11, **30–31**, 43, 102
  Nezu Shrine 42
  Nogi Shrine 95, 97
  Sumiyoshi Shrine 16
  Suwa Shrine 32
  Togo Shrine 102
  Toshogu Shrine 20
  Toyokawa Inari Betsuin 96
  water purification rites 71
  Yasukuni Shrine 42–3, 77
  see also Temples
Shunmyo, Masuno 48
Sompo J Museum of Art 108
Spiral 46, 103
Starck, Philippe 16, 50
Stone Age Tokyo 27
Street art
  Roppongi 96
Streetcars 52
Subway 122
Suginami Animation Museum 116
Sumida River 6, 7, 10, **16–17**, 89
  fireworks 17, 71
Sumiyoshi Shrine 16
Suntory Hall 58
Suntory Museum of Art 95, 97
Suwa Shrine 32

T

Taisho period 83
Taka Ishii Gallery 47
Takamori 21
Takamura, Koun 27
Takao, Mount 114
Takarazuka Theater 58
Takashimaya Times Square 108–9
Takeshita-dori 7, 102

Tange, Kenzo 35, 50, 51, 102, 103, 109
Taniguchi, Yoshio 26
Tanizaki, Junichiro 39
Taro Okamoto Memorial Museum 103
Tatsuno, Kingo 40, 41, 75, 76
Taxis 122
Tea ceremony 29
Telephones 126
Temples 68
  Benten-do 21
  Gokuku-ji Temple 41
  Hongan-ji Temple 40
  Jindaiji Temple 116
  Kotozan Daien-ji Temple 32
  Naritasan Shinsho-ji Temple 115
  Sengaku-ji Temple 42
  Senso-ji Temple 6, 7, 8–9, 10, **14–15**, 38, 42, 88, 89
  Tenno-ji Temple 32
  Toyokawa Inari Betsuin 96
  Yushima Seido Temple 42
  Zensho-an Temple 32
  Zojo-ji Temple 6, 43, 97
  see also Shrines
Tenno-ji Temple 32
Terrorism 39
Theaters 58–9
  Kabuki-za Theater 6, 59, 81
Theme parks *see* Amusement parks
Themed Cafés 53
Time zone 126
Tipping 126
Toden Arakawa Tram Line 52
Togo, Admiral Heihachiro 102
Togo, Seiji 108
Togo Shrine 102
Toguri Museum of Art 102
Tokudaiji Sahei 28
Tokugawa, Ieyasu 20, 38, 113
Tokugawa shogunate 28, 43, 97
Tokugawa, Yorifusa 28
Tokugawa, Yoshinobu 32
Tokyo Big Sight 35, 56
Tokyo City View 97
Tokyo Disney® Resort 55, 116
Tokyo Dome 59
Tokyo Dome City 55
Tokyo International Forum 7, 49, 82
Tokyo Marathon 70
Tokyo Metropolitan Art Museum 87
Tokyo Metropolitan Government Building 7, 48, 109
Tokyo Metropolitan Museum of Photography 45
Tokyo Midtown 6, 95, 97
Tokyo National Museum 6, 7, 11, **24–7**, 45, 87
Tokyo Skytree 6, 7, 17, 49, 89
Tokyo Station 7, 41, 76, 77
Tokyo Tower 6, 96
Tomei Onsen Sakura 60
The Tolman Collection 46
Torii 30
Toshogu Shrine 20
Tourist information 126–7
Tours 69
Toyokan 26
Toyokawa Inari Betsuin 96
Toyosu Fish Market 66
Trains 120, 121
  Railway Museum (Omiya) 54, 113
Trams 122
Travel 69, 120–23
Travelers with specific requirements 125
Travel insurance 124
Travel safety advice 124
Tsukiji Outer Market 6, 66, 82
Tsukuda-jima 16
Tsunayoshi 42
Tsutenkyo Bridge 29
Tyffonium 34

U

Ueno, Asakusa, and Oshiage **86–91**
  maps 86–7, 89
  restaurants 91
  specialist shops 90
  walk 89
Ueno, Battle of (1868) 33
Ueno, Professor 101
Ueno Park 6, 7, 10, **20–21**, 86
Ueno Sakuragi Atari 33
Ueno Zoo 20
Ugolini 30
Umaya Bridge 17
United Nations University 103
Yonehara, Unkai 27

V

Van Gogh, Vincent 108
Viewing observatories 68
Viñoly, Rafael 51, 82
Visas 124
Visitor information 126–7

W

Wadakura Fountain Park 13
Wako Building 41
Walks
  Aoyama, Harajuku, and Shibuya 103
  Central Tokyo 77
  Ginza 83
  Roppongi and Akasaka 97
  Shinjuku 109
  Ueno, Asakusa, and Oshiage 89
  walking tours 69
Watanabe, Jin 26, 41
Water parks
  Wadakura Fountain Park 13
Water purification rites 71
Weather 126
Wi-Fi 69
Women travelers 125
World War II 13, 39
Wright, Frank Lloyd 52

Y

Yanagi Bridge 16
Yanaka 7, 11, **32–3**
Yanaka Cemetery 32
Yanaka Ginza 32
Yasukuni Shrine 42–3, 77
Yayoi Kusama Museum 44, 107
Yokohama 114, 118–19
Yoyogi National Gymnasium 102
Yoyogi Park 51, 68–9
Yushima Seido Temple 42

Z

Zensho-an Temple 32
Zhu Shunshui 28
Zojo-ji Temple 6, 43, 97
Zoos
  Ueno Zoo 20

Acknowledgments

This edition updated by

Contributor Rob Goss
Senior Editor Alison McGill
Senior Designer Stuti Tiwari
Project Editors Parnika Bagla, Zoë Rutland
Assistant Editor Anjasi N.N.
Art Editor Ankita Sharma
Picture Research Administrator Vagisha Pushp
Publishing Assistant Halima Mohammed
Jacket Designer Jordan Lambley
Senior Cartographer Ashif
Cartography Manager Suresh Kumar
DTP Designer Rohit Rojal
Senior Production Editor Jason Little
Production Controller Manjit Sihra
Deputy Managing Editor Beverly Smart
Managing Editors Shikha Kulkarni, Hollie Teague
Managing Art Editor Sarah Snelling
Senior Managing Art Editor Priyanka Thakur
Art Director Maxine Pedliham
Publishing Director Georgina Dee

DK would like to thank the following for their contribution to the previous editions: Stephen Mansfield, Simon Richmond, Bill Willis, Leena Lane, Hilary Bird

The publisher would like to thank the following for their kind permission to reproduce their photographs:
Key: a-above; b-below/bottom; c-centre; f-far; l-left; r-right; t-top

123RF.com: Kriengkrai Choochote 112tl; coward_lion 21c; Ivan Marchuk 74tl; sean pavone 20-1c, 106cl; Norikazu Satomi 10clb; yyama3270 16bl.

3331 Arts Chiyoda: Chiyoda Arts Festival 2011 47cr.

Alamy Stock Photo: A.F. Archive 59br; AFLO/ Nippon News/Natsuki Sakai 71cla; Aflo Co. Ltd 71bc; Andia / Benard 61tr; /Keiki Haginoya 31br; age fotostock/Javier Larrea 42b; Mark Bassett 4cr; Masayuki Yamashita 75br; Patrick Batchelder 3tl, 72-3; Paul Brown 92-3; Songquan Deng 15bl; World Discovery 32cl, 47t, 67tr, 67cl, 78cla, 104clb; EDU Vision 52tl, 76br; F1online digitale Bildagentur GmbH /S. Tauqueur 11br; Matt Fagg 34br; Gavin Hellier 69cl; Peter Horree 24cr; Alex Hunter 51tl; INTERFOTO/Fine Arts 45tl, /History 38br; Japan Stock Photography 77tl; JTB MEDIA CREATION, Inc /JTB Photo/UIG 11clb, 40cl, 96t; Andrey Kekyalyaynen 14clb; Hideo Kurihara 18bc; John Lander 28br, 29tl; Yannick Luthy 114bl; Oleksiy Maksymenko 49b, 55tr; Greg McNevin 53cl; Luciano Mortula 43cr; Motion/Horizon Images 70tl; James Nesterwitz 32br; Newscom / BJ Warnick 66br; NPC Collectiom 10crb; Sean Pavone, 17tl, 34-5, 57clb, 68cla, 103tl; PersimmonPictures.com 52b; Phanie/Voisin 57tr; Prisma Bildagentur AG/Raga Jose Fuste 13cr, 56br; Alex Segre 66tl, 69tr; John Steele 94tl; Jeremy Sutton-Hibbert 63b; Ivan Vdovin 27ca; Steve Vidler 88tl; Peter M. Wilson 11cr; World Discovery 19tl, 44clb; Masayuki Yamashita 50cl.

Asakusa Imahan: 62t.

AWL Images: Christian Kober 117cra; Matteo Colombo 1; Travel Pix Collection 2tl, 8-9.

Bridgeman Images: Seiji Togo Memorial Sompo Japan Nipponkoa Museum of Art, Tokyo, Japan *Sunflowers* (1889) by Vincent van Gogh 108tr; Werner Forman Archive 80tl.

Codename MIXOLOGY Akasaka: 98b.

Corbis: 39br; All Canada Photos/Ken Paul 15cr; Atlantide Phototravel /Massimo Borchi 12br, 75t, 82-3, 111bl; Bettmann 39cl; Tibor Bognar 86tr; incamerastock /Iain Masterton, 95cra; Masterfile /F. Lukasseck 96br; Nippon News/AFLO 102cl; Photononstop /Calle Montes 109cl.

Design Festa: 70cr.

Dreamstime.com: Andreevaee 89cl; Bennnn 115cla; Bennymarty 50bl, 71tr; Ratchadaporn Chullanan 30cla; Cowardlion 20br, 41tl, 54b, 76tl, 86cl, 97cl, 102b, 113t; dragoncello 31tl; Esmehelit 60b; Foto99 95b; Fotokon 46bl; Gjeerawut 87tr; Hiro1775 49tl, 114cl; Javarman 107b; Mihai-bogdan Lazar 6cla; Esteban Miyahira 113br; Mnsanthoshkumar 79bl; Luciano Mortula 7cra, 14-5; Sean Pavone 6t, 10cla, 40b, 82tl; Jaturun Phuengphuttharak 4cla; Ppy2010ha 105crb; Siraanamwong 100cla; Tktktk 54cla; Torsakarin 51bl; Maria Vazquez 88b; Sarah Wilkie 5clb; Buddhapong Wongsanont 10c; Xiye 31clb; Yuryz 55clb, 68b.

Getty Images: AFP/Reuters/Issei Kato 59cla; AFP / Kazuhiro Nogi 56t; AFP / Charly Triballeau 85bl; /Toshifumi Kitamura 58tl; AFP / Yoshikazu Tsuno 65b; Aro @ Photography 15crb; Marco Brivio 12-3; Print Collector 38cla; JTB Photo 17crb; Koichi Kamoshida 58crb; LightRocket/John S Lander 27b, 28cla; Sergio Lora 11crb, 32-3; takau99 29crb; UIG/JTB Photo 16-7, 101t.

Goodbeer Faucets: 65t.

iStockphoto.com: coward_lion 4t; helovi 35crb; Hiro1775 116b; ke 3tr, 118-9; magicflute002 2tr, 14cla, 36-7b; MiriamPolito 42cla; orpheus26 30-1; Marek Slusarczyk 10b; shirophoto 4b; Thananat 21tl; winhorse 53tr, 81b.

Mori Art Musem: 45b.

National Film Center Exhibition: 81tr.

National Museum of Emerging Science and Innovation: 35tr.

The National Museum of Modern Art, Tokyo: *Mother and Child* (1934) by Uemura Shoen, color on silk, framed, 168.0 × 115.5 cm, Important Cultural Property 12cl.

NTT InterCommunication Center: 108bl.

Park Hyatt Tokyo: 64cl,111tr.

Photoshot: 90t.

Robert Harding Picture Library: Tibor Bognar 94cra; Lucas Vallecillos 4crb, 104tr.

Shutterstock.com: Manuel Ascanio 19clb; Hit1912 18-19c; show999 22-23

Images courtesy of Tokyo National Museum: 11tl, 24bl, 25tl, 25bc, 25clb, 26t, 26clb, 45c.

Watering Hole: 110cl.

Cover

Front and spine: **Getty Images:** DigitalVision / Matteo Colombo.

Back: **Dreamstime.com:** F11photo tr, Natalia Lisovskaya crb, Nathapon Triratanachat tl; **AWL Images:** Marco Bottigelli cla; **Getty Images:** DigitalVision / Matteo Colombo b.

Pull Out Map Cover

Getty Images: DigitalVision / Matteo Colombo.

All other images © Dorling Kindersley

For further information see: www.dkimages.com

DK | Penguin Random House

First edition 2009

First published in Great Britain by Dorling Kindersley Limited, DK, One Embassy Gardens, 8 Viaduct Gardens, London SW11 7BW, UK

The authorised representative in the EEA is Dorling Kindersley Verlag GmbH. Arnulfstr. 124, 80636 Munich, Germany

Published in the United States by DK Publishing, 1745 Broadway, 20th Floor, New York, NY 10019, USA

24 25 10 9 8 7 6

A CIP catalog record is available from the British Library.

A catalog record for this book is available from the Library of Congress.

ISSN 1479-344X

ISBN 978-0-2416-1219-4

Printed and bound in China

www.dk.com

As a guide to abbreviations in visitor information blocks: ***Adm*** *= admission charge*

MIX
Paper | Supporting responsible forestry
FSC
www.fsc.org
FSC™ C018179

This book was made with Forest Stewardship Council™ certified paper – one small step in DK's commitment to a sustainable future.
For more information go to www.dk.com/our-green-pledge

Phrase Book

The origins of the Japanese language are unclear. Written Japanese uses a combination of four scripts: Chinese ideograms, known as *kanji*; two syllable-based alphabet systems known as *hiragana* and *katakana*; and the Latin alphabet, *romaji*. *Hiragana* and *katakana* are similar, *katakana* often functioning to transcribe non-Japanese words. Traditionally, Japanese is written in vertical columns from top right to bottom left, though the Western system is widely used. There are several romanization systems: the Hepburn system is used in this guide. To simplify romanization, macrons (long marks over vowels to indicate longer pronunciation) have not been used. Japanese pronunciation is fairly straightforward, and many words are "Japanized" versions of Western words. This Phrase Book gives the English word or phrase, followed by the Japanese script, then the romanization, adapted to aid pronunciation.

Guidelines for Pronunciation

When reading the romanization, give the same emphasis to all syllables. The practice in English of giving one syllable greater stress may render a Japanese word incomprehensible.

Pronounce vowels as in these English words:

a	*as the "a" in "again"*
e	*as in "red"*
i	*as in "in"*
o	*as in "solid"*
u	*as the "u" in "cuckoo"*

When two vowels are used together, sound each letter separately:

ai	*as in "pine"*
ae	*as if written "ah-eh"*
ei	*as in "pay"*

Consonants are pronounced as in English. The letter *g* is always hard as in "gate," and *j* is always soft as in "joke." *R* is pronounced something between *r* and l. *F* is sometimes pronounced as *h*. *"Si"* always becomes *"shi,"* but some people pronounce *"shi"* as *"hi." V* in Western words (e.g., "video") becomes *b*. If followed by a consonant, *n* may be pronounced as either *n* or *m*.

All consonants except *n* are always either followed by a vowel or doubled; however, sometimes an *i* or *u* is barely pronounced. In this Phrase Book, to aid pronunciation, apostrophes are used where an *i* or *u* is barely pronounced within a word, and double consonants where this occurs at the end of a word.

Dialects

Standard Japanese is used and understood throughout Japan by people of all backgrounds. But on a colloquial level, there are significant differences in both pronunciation and vocabulary, even between the Tokyo and Osaka-Kyoto areas, and rural accents are very strong.

Polite Words and Phrases

There are several different levels of politeness in the Japanese language, according to status, age, and situation. In everyday conversation, politeness levels are simply a question of the length of verb endings (longer is more polite), but in formal conversation entirely different words (*keigo*) are used. The level given in this Phrase Book is neutral, yet polite.

In an Emergency

Help!	たすけて！	*Tas'kete!*
Stop!	とめて！	*Tomete!*
Call a doctor!	医者をよんでください！	*Isha o yonde kudasai!*
Call an ambulance!	救急車をよんでください！	*Kyukyusha o yonde kudasai!*
Call the police!	警察をよんでください！	*Keisatsu o yonde kudasai!*
Fire!	火事！	*Kaji!*
Where is the hospital?	病院はどこにありますか？	*Byoin wa doko ni arimass-ka?*
police box	交番	*koban*

Communication Essentials

Yes/no.	はい／いいえ	*Hai/ie.*
Thank you.	ありがとう。	*Arigato.*
Please (offering).	どうぞ。	*Dozo.*
Please (asking).	おねがいします。	*Onegai shimass.*
Do you speak English?	英語を話せますか？	*Eigo o hanasemass-ka?*
I can't speak Japanese.	日本語は話せません。	*Nihongo wa hanasemasen.*
Sorry/Excuse me!	すみません。	*Sumimasen!*
Could you help me please? (not emergency)	ちょっと手伝っていただけませんか？	*Chotto tets'datte itadakemasen-ka?*

Useful Phrases

My name is…	わたしの名前は･･･です。	*Watashi no namae wa… dess.*
How do you do, pleased to meet you.	はじめまして、どうぞよろしく。	*Hajime-mash'te dozo yorosh'ku.*
How are you?	お元気ですか？	*Ogenki dess-ka?*
Good morning.	おはようございます。	*Ohayo gozaimass.*
Good afternoon/good day.	こんにちは。	*Konnichiwa.*
Good evening.	こんばんは。	*Konbanwa.*
Good night.	おやすみなさい。	*Oyasumi nasai.*
Good-bye.	さよなら。	*Sayonara.*
What is (this)?	（これは）何ですか？	*(Kore wa) nan dess-ka?*
Where can I get …?	･･･はどこにありますか？	*…wa doko ni arimass-ka?*
How much is it?	いくらですか？	*Ikura dess-ka?*
What time is …?	･･･何時ですか？	*… nan-ji dess-ka?*
Cheers! (toast)	乾杯！	*Kanpai!*
Where is the restroom/toilet?	お手洗い／おトイレはどこですか？	*Toire wa doko dess-ka?*
Here's my business card.	名刺をどうぞ。	*Meishi o dozo.*
How do you use this?	これをどうやって使いますか？	*Kore o doyatte ts'kaimass-ka?*

Useful Words

I	わたし	*watashi*
woman	女性	*josei*
man	男性	*dansei*
wife	奥さん	*ok'san*
husband	主人	*shujin*
big/small	大きい／小さい	*okii/chiisai*
hot/cold	暑い／寒い	*atsui/samui*
warm	温かい	*atatakai*
good/not good/bad	いい／よくない／悪い	*ii/yokunai/warui*
free (no charge)	ただ／無料	*tada/muryo*
here	ここ	*koko*
there	あそこ	*asoko*
this	これ	*kore*

that (nearby)	それ	*sore*
that (far away)	あれ	*are*
what?	何？	*nani?*
when?	いつ？	*itsu?*
why?	なぜ？／どうして？	*naze?/dosh'te?*
where?	どこ？	*doko?*
who?	誰？	*dare?*
which way?	どちら？	*dochira?*
enough	じゅうぶん／結構	*jubun/kekko*

Signs

open	営業中	*eigyo-chu*
closed	休日	*kyujitsu*
entrance	入口	*iriguchi*
exit	出口	*deguchi*
danger	危険	*kiken*
emergency exit	非常口	*hijo-guchi*
information	案内	*annai*
restroom, toilet	お手洗い／手洗い／おトイレ／トイレ	*otearai/tearai/otoire/toire*
free (vacant)	空き	*aki*
men	男	*otoko*
women	女	*onna*

Money

Could you change this into yen please.	これを円に替えてください。	*Kore o en ni kaete kudasai.*
I'd like to cash these travelers' checks.	このトラベラーズチェックを現金にしたいです。	*Kono toraberazu chekku o genkin ni shitai dess.*
Do you take credit cards/travelers' checks?	クレジットカード／トラベラーズチェックで払えますか？	*Kurejitto kado/toraberazu chekku de haraemass-ka?*
bank	銀行	*ginko*
cash	現金	*genkin*
credit card	クレジットカード	*kurejitto kado*
currency exchange office	両替所	*ryogaejo*
dollars	ドル	*doru*
pounds	ポンド	*pondo*
yen	円	*en*

Keeping in Touch

Where is a telephone?	電話はどこにありますか	*Denwa wa doko ni arimass-ka?*
May I use your phone?	電話を使ってもいいですか	*Denwa o ts'katte mo ii dess-ka?*
Hello, this is ….	もしもし、…です。	*Moshi-moshi, … dess.*
I'd like to make an international call.	国際電話、お願いします	*Kokusai denwa, onegai shimass.*
airmail	航空便	*kokubin*
email	メール	*me-ru*
fax	ファクス	*fak'su*
postcard	ハガキ	*hagaki*
post office	郵便局	*yubin-kyoku*
stamp	切手	*kitte*
telephone booth	公衆電話	*koshu denwa*
telephone card	テレフォンカード	*terefon kado*

Staying in a Hotel

Do you have any vacancies?	部屋がありますか？	*Heya ga arimass-ka?*
I have a reservation.	予約をしてあります。	*Yoyaku o sh'te arimass.*
I'd like a room with a bathroom.	お風呂つきの部屋、お願いします。	*Ofuro-ts'ki no heya, onegai shimass.*
What is the charge per night?	一泊いくらですか？	*Ippaku ikura dess-ka?*
Japanese-style inn	旅館	*ryokan*
Japanese-style room	和室	*wa-shitsu*
key	鍵	*kagi*
front desk	フロント	*furonto*
single/twin room	シングル／ツイ	*shinguru/tsuin*
shower	シャワー	*shawa*
Western-style hotel	ホテル	*hoteru*
Western-style room	洋室	*yo-shitsu*
Is tax included in the price?	税込みですか？	*Zeikomi dess-ka?*
Can I leave my luggage here for a little while?	荷物をちょっとここに預けてもいいですか？	*Nimotsu o chotto koko ni azukete mo ii dess-ka?*
air-conditioning	冷房／エアコン	*reibo/eakon*
bath	お風呂	*ofuro*
check-out	チェックアウト	*chekku-auto*

Eating Out

A table for one/two/three, please.	一人／二人／三人、お願いします。	*Hitori/futari/sannin, onegai shimass.*
May I see the menu.	メニュー、お願いします。	*Menyu, onegai shimass.*
Is there a set menu?	定食がありますか？	*Teishoku ga arimass-ka?*
I'd like ….	私は…がいいです。	*Watashi wa … ga ii dess.*
May I have one of those?	それをひとつ、お願いします。	*Sore o hitotsu, onegai shimass.*
I am a vegetarian.	私はベジタリアンです。	*Watashi wa bejitarian dess.*
Waiter/waitress!	ちょっとすみません。	*Chotto sumimasen!*
What would you recommend?	おすすめは何ですか？	*Osusume wa nan dess-ka?*
How do you eat this?	これはどうやって食べますか？	*Kore wa doyatte tabemass-ka?*
May we have the check please.	お勘定、お願いします。	*Okanjo, onegai shimass.*
May we have some more …	もっと…、お願いします。	*Motto …, onegai shimass.*
The meal was very good, thank you.	ごちそうさまでした、おいしかったです。	*Gochiso-sama desh'ta, oishikatta dess.*
assortment	盛りあわせ	*moriawase*
boxed meal	弁当	*bento*
breakfast	朝食	*cho-shoku*
buffet	バイキング	*baikingu*
delicious	おいしい	*oishii*
dinner	夕食	*yu-shoku*
to drink	飲む	*nomu*
a drink	飲みもの	*nomimono*
to eat	食べる	*taberu*
food	食べもの／ごはん	*tabemono/gohan*
full (stomach)	おなかがいっぱい	*onaka ga ippai*
hot/cold	熱い／冷たい	*atsui/tsumetai*
hungry	おなかがすいた	*onaka ga suita*
Japanese food	和食	*wa-shoku*
lunch	昼食	*chu-shoku*
set menu	セット／定食	*setto (snack)/teishoku (meal)*
spicy	辛い	*karai*
sweet, mild	甘い	*amai*
Western food	洋食	*yo-shoku*
pepper	こしょう	*kosho*
salt	塩	*shio*
vegetables	野菜	*yasai*
sugar	砂糖	*sato*